The Manner of Giving

Studies of the East Asian Institute—Columbia University

The East Asian Institute of Columbia University

The East Asian Institute is Columbia University's center for research, publication, and teaching on modern East Asia. The Studies of the East Asian Institute were inaugurated in 1962 to bring to a wider public the results of significant new research on Japan, China, and Korea.

The Manner of Giving

Strategic Aid and Japanese Foreign Policy

Dennis T. Yasutomo
Smith College

Lexington Books
D.C. Heath and Company/Lexington, Massachusetts/Toronto

Library of Congress Cataloging-in-Publication Data

Yasutomo, Dennis T.
    The manner of giving.

    (Studies of the East Asian Institute, Columbia University)
    Bibliography: p.
    Includes index.
    1. Economic assistance, Japanese—Developing countries.   2. Japan—Foreign
economic relations.   I. Title. II. Series: Studies of the East Asian Institute.
HC60.Y37 1986   338.91'52'01724   85-46026
ISBN 0-669-12894-5 (alk. paper)

Published simultaneously in Canada
Printed in the United States of America
Casebound International Standard Book Number: 0-669-12894-5
Library of Congress Catalog Card Number: 85-46026

The paper used in this publication meets the minimum requirements of American National
Standard for Information Sciences—Permanence of Paper for Printed Library Materials,
ANSI Z39.48-1984.
    ∞ ™

The last numbers on the right below indicate the number and date of printing.

10   9   8   7   6   5   4   3   2   1

95   94   93   92   91   90   89   88   87   86

To Maura, Deirdre, and Siobhan

Contents

List of Tables

Acknowledgments

T his study would not have been possible without the cooperation of numerous institutions and individuals, most of whom are listed under Interviews and Assistance in the bibliography. The Social Science Research Council and American Council of Learned Societies, with funding provided by the U.S.-Japan Friendship Commission, provided a generous research grant for a one-year stay in Tokyo during the 1982–1983 academic year.

The Institute of Developing Economies (*Ajia Keizai Kenkyujo*) served as my host institution during my time in Japan, appointing me as a visiting research fellow. I was able to renew old and make new friendships at "Ajiken" as well as conduct research. Their names are too numerous to list here, but their generous assistance will never be forgotten. I would especially like to cite the kindness of the International Exchanges Department and Matsumoto Shigekazu, director of the Economic Cooperation Department, who provided advice and much assistance in wandering through the maze of Japan's aid policy. Sakumoto Naoyuki and Tsuneishi Takao made research easier and enjoyable. In addition, I would also like to thank the other visiting research fellows, most of whom came from developing nations, for their willingness to teach me so much about their homelands.

Once again, I owe a tremendous debt of gratitude to the East Asian Institute of Columbia University, especially to its director, James William Morley. He read the first and final drafts of this study, and his understanding of and insight into Japanese foreign policy continue to impress and inspire me. Gerald Curtis, Herbert Passin, Richard Sneider, Jack Bresnan, and Robert Jervis—all of Columbia—commented or assisted on some aspect of this project at the initial stages. Robert Ross oversaw the process that led to this book's publication.

I would also like to express appreciation to several other individuals for their cooperation: Skipp Orr, Nishihara Masashi, Nozaki Seigo, Matsuura Koichiro, Nogami Yoshiji, and Sakurai Toshihiro. I owe a special debt of gratitude to Susan Pharr for her comments and advice.

I began this project as a research associate at Columbia's East Asian Institute. I assumed my current position at Smith College upon my return from Japan. The study was completed at Smith, a task greatly facilitated by the congenial atmosphere in the Five College area among faculty colleagues, friends, and students.

Needless to say, the final responsibility for opinions and conclusions in this book rests with me, not with the above-named individuals or institutions.

Finally, all Asian names in the text will appear in the Asian style, with surnames preceding given names.

The manner of giving
is worth more than the gift.

—Pierre Corneille

1
Economic Assistance and Japanese Foreign Policy

Japan is ready to become, by completely changing its heretofore passive attitude, a nation which will actively fulfill its international responsibility to strengthen and promote world peace and development. From a passive beneficiary to an active creator—This, I might say, is the third start for our country.

—Prime Minister Suzuki Zenko

Japan's ODA is intended to help the developing countries in their self-help efforts for economic and social development, improvement of the people's welfare. We believe such assistance is conducive to enhanced political, economic and social resiliency of developing countries, and in the long run contributes to world peace and stability....ODA is recognized to be an important international responsibility, appropriate for a country committed to world peace and enjoying the second largest economy in the free world.

—From *Japan's Official Development Assistance 1984 Annual Report*

The Japanese may be mortals after all. The pace of postwar Japan's spectacular "economic miracle" has slowed from the torrid 10 percent average annual GNP growth rate of the 1960s to a "mere" 4 to 6 percent in the late 1970s and early 1980s. Since 1981 the government has embarked on policies of fiscal reconstruction and administrative reform designed to improve government efficiency and reduce public sector spending. The 1982 national budget recorded the lowest rate of expansion in 26 years (at 6.2%), and the 1984 budget revealed a nominal expansion (0.5%). Budget austerity has hit hardest at social welfare expenditures. In 1984 social welfare spending increased by only 2 percent, education and science by 1 percent, and energy by 0.9 percent, while pensions decreased by 0.26 percent, small business expenditures by 5.5 percent, and public works by 2 percent.[1]

In an era of fiscal austerity and zero-growth national budgets, when the Japanese government forces belt-tightening measures on its own people, one budget item has been extended special treatment and exempted from severe spending cuts—money for foreign aid. While domestic social infrastructure spending stagnated, Japan's economic assistance has enjoyed comparatively explosive annual increases (12.8% in 1981, 11.4% in 1982, 8.9% in 1983, 9.7% in

1984, and 10% in 1985). Foreign aid budgets now expand faster each year than any other item, an average increase of 10 percent per annum between 1981 and 1985. Only one other budget item comes close to matching the aid budget's record—defense spending, the other item exempted from the minus ceiling guidelines. But even annual defense expenditure increases fall short of aid budget hikes (7.6% in 1981, 7.8% in 1982, 6.5% in 1983, 6.65% in 1984, and 6.9% in 1985).[2] Japan is one nation where foreign aid expenditures expand more rapidly than defense spending. Overall, between 1981 and 1985, Official Development Assistance (ODA) enjoyed a 31.5 percent increase, defense totaled 21 percent, social welfare spending crawled upward to 5 percent, while education, culture, and science and technology stagnated at 0.5 percent.[3]

The emphasis on economic and technical assistance to developing nations at a time of domestic economic difficulties is striking for a nation lacking any notable humanitarian or philanthropic tradition toward outsiders. It comes at a time when the premier aid-giver in the world, the United States, has downplayed the usefulness of aid for economic development. The Ronald Reagan administration has favored private flows and has urged developing nations to rely on the "magic of the marketplace." It has shown less faith in multilateral financial institutions, putting them on notice soon after taking office that they must survive on smaller contributions from Washington.[4]

In contrast with the current U.S. attitude and approach, successive Japanese cabinets have affirmed and reaffirmed their belief in the critical role of ODA in sparking Third World development and, thereby, economic recovery in the developed world. In the words of one government official,

> Laying the foundation of growth in the developing countries through economic assistance from the industrial world will promote their steady growth. This will work to create new demand in the world economy, and function as a pillar in supporting the medium- and long-term global recovery. The industrial world should fully appreciate the fact that efforts to reflate the national economies and aid the Third World will revitalize and open up the frontiers of the world economy. At this moment, when the world economy is suffering from a persistent recession, the industrial countries must expand and improve their economic cooperation to the Third World.[5]

The government doubled aid outflows between 1977 and 1980 from $1.4 billion to $3.3 billion in annual disbursements. In 1981 the Suzuki Zenko cabinet pledged another doubling in five years. By using aggregate spending for the last half of the 1970s as its base ($10.7 billion), Tokyo vowed to reach an aggregate spending target of $21.4 billion by the end of fiscal year 1985, and to increase aid as a proportion of GNP far beyond the 0.32 percent of 1980.[6]

The fiscal austerity policy, foreign exchange rate fluctuations, recipient nations' absorptive capabilities, and other problems prevented the Japanese from fulfilling the aid-doubling pledge.[7] Nevertheless, Japan's performance in the 1980s catapulted Tokyo in 1983 to the status of the third largest donor nation, and in 1984 Tokyo surpassed France to become number two.

In the field of multilateral assistance, Japan remains the largest contributor to the Asian Development Bank and a strong supporter of the United Nations and its specialized agencies. It joined the African Development Fund in 1973 and became a full member of the African Development Bank in 1983. Japan has been active in the Inter-American Development Bank since it gained membership in 1976.[8] In mid-1984 Tokyo became the second largest supplier of funds to the World Bank.

In September 1985 the cabinet approved its third consecutive aid-doubling plan. The government established an aggregate spending total for bilateral and multilateral ODA of $40 billion by 1992. Annual aid outflow is expected to reach $8 billion, constituting a record 0.42 percent of GNP.[9] If successful, the Japanese will have attained the current annual aid outlay of the United States. And should U.S. foreign aid expenditures stagnate or increase only gradually, Japan can conceivably become the premier aid-giver in the world by the next century.

Perhaps the greatest anomaly of Japan's foreign aid policy in the view of foreign observers is the overwhelming support among the majority of the populace for foreign aid. While "aid fatigue" afflicts citizens of many other donor nations, public opinion polls in Japan taken between 1977 and 1981 register a consistent 75 to 80 percent support rate. A recent poll reveals that close to 40 percent of the people support an expansion of aid to developing nations.[10] All political parties, from the conservative ruling party to the centrist and leftist opposition forces, join together each year to approve the economic cooperation budget in the National Diet. Big business, organized labor, the bureaucracy, and the mass media all take favorable and enthusiastic positions on money for foreign countries. Japan's foreign aid policy apparently rests on the bedrock of support and consensus.

Even critics of Japanese aid policy focus not on the desirability of aid but on the paucity of the amount and the harshness of the terms and conditions. Japanese critics want better, not less, economic assistance. They look at other statistics and find Japanese performance wanting.

> Any Japanese who has taken a look at international statistics on economic assistance should be shocked to learn how poor Japan's performance has been in the past. Take any relevant statistic: The ratio of official development assistance to GNP, the ratio of untied assistance to total assistance, or the proportion of "grant element" in the total assistance. According to any of these indicators, Japanese performance has been among the worst in the OECD (Organization for Economic Cooperation and Development).[11]

In the 1980s, however, the significance of Japan's aid activities lies not only in amounts, terms and conditions, and ratios or percentages, all of which have been improving. Its significance rests in the government's explicit designation of ODA as a foreign policy tool for achieving political and security objectives as well as economic benefits. The past three cabinets (Ohira Masayoshi, 1978–1980; Suzuki Zenko, 1980–1982); and Nakasone Yasuhiro, 1982–present) have added a strategic dimension to Japan's traditional economic aid policy. Japan has substantially increased aid to such diverse and geographically dispersed nations as Oman, Sudan, Turkey, Pakistan, Zimbabwe, South Korea, North Yemen, Jamaica, Somalia, Kenya, the People's Republic of China, Egypt, and the members of the Association of Southeast Asian Nations (ASEAN: Thailand, Malaysia, the Philippines, Indonesia, Singapore, and, as of 1984, Brunei). Not all of these nations possess deep economic ties to Japan, but all are considered critical for the security interests of the Western alliance.

In addition, Japan has taken an unusually decisive step by utilizing economic assistance as a diplomatic sanction. Tokyo has reduced or withheld aid to the Socialist Republic of Vietnam, Kampuchea (Cambodia), Cuba, Angola, Afghanistan, and Ethiopia for political reasons.[12] Japan has apparently taken a step away from its traditional approach of "separating politics from economics" (*seikei bunri*), devised by the Ikeda Hayato cabinet (1960–1964) to apply to trade relations with the People's Republic of China in the absence of formal diplomatic relations.

Japan has inaugurated a policy of extending, or denying, economic assistance for strategic purposes to nations deemed important to international as well as to Japanese peace and security. The government's exemption of both economic cooperation and defense from the budget austerity policy in the 1980s can now be seen in a new light: The aid and defense budgets and policies are related. The growing visibility of aid policy parallels the evolution of a heightened defense consciousness among the Japanese government and people, especially since the fall of Saigon in 1975. A growing majority now accept the constitutionality of and necessity for the Self-Defense Force (SDF), support the U.S.-Japan Security Treaty and show greater willingness to discuss even the most sensitive of defense issues. The government has exhibited greater willingness to cooperate with the United States in maintaining defense, by participating in joint military exercises, increased responsibility for sea surveillance, transfer of military technology, policy coordination, and agreement to cooperate in blockading of the straits surrounding Japan (Tsugaru, Soya, and Tsushima) in times of crisis.

In foreign policy Japan has exhibited greater activism and assertiveness since the late 1970s. It joined the boycott of the 1980 Olympics in Moscow and instituted economic sanctions against the Soviet Union following the invasion of Afghanistan; it froze aid to Vietnam after the invasion and occupation of Kampuchea and strongly backed anti-Vietnamese diplomatic efforts by ASEAN in the United Nations; it instituted economic sanctions against Iran for the taking of American hostages in 1979; it refused economic assistance to Poland for the treatment of the labor union Solidarity; it concluded a Treaty of Peace and Friendship with China, much to Moscow's chagrin; and it forged a closer relationship with South Korea in recognition of Seoul's strategic importance to Japan. Economic aid played a major role in many of these diplomatic moves, either in support of specific countries or as sanctions. Greater activism in aid and defense policies and in overall foreign policy seem to run parallel.

Greater defense consciousness and foreign activism do not signal a trend toward a revival of Japanese militarism. The defense debate does not focus solely on military aspects of national security. The underpinning of current security policy is the concept of "comprehensive national security" (*sogo anzen hosho*), developed at the urging of Prime Minister Ohira Masayoshi in 1979–1980, adopted by Prime Minister Suzuki Zenko as national policy in 1980, and endorsed by Prime Minister Nakasone Yasuhiro in 1982. Comprehensive security is a long-range view of the nation's security requirements that blends recognition of both military and nonmilitary threats to the nation and the need for both military and nonmilitary countermeasures. In theory the concept balances the importance of both types of threats and responses, which range from strengthening the SDF's "denial force" against military aggression to securing stable sources of foodstuffs and energy resources. Economic aid's principal function is to serve as a deterrent to the rise of nonmilitary threats against the nation by creating a stable and favorable international environment.[13] As the *Diplomatic Bluebook* notes, "The most important thing for comprehensive national security policy ... is to always keep our external environment as peaceful and stable as possible, thereby preventing crises from arising. This is precisely the basic task of our foreign policy."[14]

In the 1980s foreign aid policy has emerged as the centerpiece of comprehensive security's nonmilitary components and a central pillar of overall foreign policy. The foundation of aid policy no longer appears to be a one-dimensional concern for economic gain. Three major developments characterize Japanese aid policy since the late 1970s:

1. Politicization of its rationale to include strategic as well as economic objectives

2. Globalization of its scope beyond the traditional concentration on the Asian region

3. Improvements in the quantity and quality of aid

The third development includes aid-doubling plans, untying efforts, attention to the poorest nations and basic human needs rather than large-scale industrial projects, improvements in terms and conditions, and greater attention to aid evaluation and effectiveness.

This book focuses primarily on the politicization and globalization of aid policy and on the reasons behind the increase in quantity. It is not a study of overall aid policy; nor does it focus in detail on Third World development or on Japan's impact on all aid recipients, although the study does raise some questions about the long-term effectiveness of strategic aid. The central focus remains the aspect not analyzed in detail by any study of Japanese aid policy: the concepts, doctrines, and theories behind strategic aid policy and its role in Japanese foreign policy. The objective is to dissect what the Japanese are trying to accomplish through the use of aid policy and why.

Aid's rise to prominence confronts interested observers with five sets of questions:

1. Why and how did strategic aid emerge and develop so quickly in view of the lingering defense allergy among the people and the usually ponderous policy-making process? How strong is the domestic consensus on aid policy, and what role does domestic politics play in shaping strategic uses of aid?

2. What is the exact relationship between economic assistance and defense policy? How, in concrete terms, is strategic aid expected to contribute to comprehensive security? Have the Japanese achieved an intergration of aid and defense policy either conceptually or in practice?

3. What effect will globalization have on Japan's traditionally regional aid focus? Does it imply less attention to Asia, including the current priority given to the ASEAN nations? Are there any limits to globalization?

4. Does strategic aid reflect indigenous Japanese interests, or is it a response to external pressure, especially from the United States? Would Japan have a strategic aid policy without outside prodding?

5. Exactly what role does strategic aid play in Japanese foreign policy, and what impact is it likely to have in the future?

The answers to these questions are basic to understanding the changing nature of Japanese foreign policy in the 1980s and beyond. One may be able to obtain a better picture of how Japan can contribute to international relations as a strong economic and moderate military power; whether Japan will refocus its diplomacy beyond Asia for noneconomic reasons; whether "independent diplomacy," a much-used slogan, is becoming a reality; and whether a domestic policy system that is often characterized as fractionated and immobilized can respond to the challenges posed by a fluid and uncertain international environment.

Japanese Aid Policy

Current interpretations of Japanese aid policy provide little help in responding to these queries. The literature tends to be outdated, pays little attention to the dimension of political security, reflects ideological biases, or attributes Japanese aid behavior to outside pressure. Many critics acknowledge the increased size and pace of Japan's recent aid flow in recent years but continue to adhere to the standard explanation, namely, economic motives. Ozawa, for example, attributes the expansion and globalization of aid policy to Japanese investment policy:

> In the 1950s, Japan's reparations program helped pave the way for the advance of Japan's trade and private overseas investments into the Asian region; in the 1960s, aid loans further opened up many markets in Asia and Latin America; and in the 1970s massive aid loans are being extended to the Middle East, accompanied by the advance of Japanese industry to the region. In fact, a greater dispersion of Japan's economic assistance has occurred since 1972—with the share of Asia declining and the share of Latin America and the Middle East rising. Yet this has happened precisely because other regions have emerged as equally important areas for Japan's overseas investment. The flows of official aid and private investment have become more concurrent than before.[15]

By focusing on economic motives, a Japanese journalist can thus argue that nothing unusual has occurred in recent aid policy:

> The deeper the business slump, the more likely it is that business will bring pressure to bear on the government to stimulate the economy in general or to bail out ailing industries by creating demand in the form of foreign aid. . . . The truth of the matter is that a substantial part of the ballooned ODA reflected the policy aim of the Japanese government to prime its own economy which was then bogged down in an oil crisis-induced recession.[16]

Japan in other words remains an "economic animal," selfishly concerned with its own rather than with the developing nations' welfare.

All literature on Japanese aid policy stresses the economic dimension. These studies conclude that economic interests determine objectives, distribution patterns, and the specific sectors of aid allocation. White basically dismisses even the existence of noneconomic criteria in his early study.[17] Caldwell places aid within the context of overall international economic development policy, while Matsui notes aid's role in a Japanese foreign economic policy characterized by the "separation of politics from economics" underpinning and an "omnidirectional" effort to remain friends with all nations.[18] Loutfi finds a Japanese concern for global peace and security for political as well as economic reasons but concludes that "their link with foreign aid is yet to be established."[19] Hasegawa concludes that Japanese aid policy aims at the attainment of national development and international ascendancy. He includes national security concerns as a third objective but dismisses its importance because of its sensitivity in domestic politics and because Japan basically entrusts its security to the United States.[20] For Rix economic aid serves as an important and integral part of Japan's economic diplomacy that helped assure Japan of market outlets and resources. Aid, he notes, "was integral to Japan's available repertoire of foreign economic policies and for some was the only diplomatic weapon Japan could use in her relations with the developing countries."[21]

Japanese aid studies rarely give prominence to political motives or security implications of ODA. Most assume their irrelevance or subordination to foreign economic policy. These works did not anticipate the rise of strategic aid and remain ill equipped to explain adequately strategic aid's birth, rationale, speed of implementation, and selection of recipient nations that do not possess deep economic ties with Japan.

The authors differ over who shapes these economic objectives. The majority point to the Japanese big business community, those with a considerable stake in the nation's export policy. These industrialists and executives of multinational firms, according to many accounts, find specific aid projects in recipient countries, shape the aid proposals submitted to their own government, and then lobby in Tokyo for the projects that would require procurement orders from these multinationals. These businesses forces are aided by influential politicians who are recruited (and amply rewarded financially for their efforts) to serve as an "aid lobby." The aid bureaucrats then accept and carry out aid allocations to these projects.[22]

A minority of analysts disagrees with this "Japan, Inc." assessment. White observes that "aid is unusual . . . in that it is not *directly* geared . . . to the interests either of the society of that nation as a whole or any segment of it, even though some interests, e.g., of exporters, may be expected to derive some adventitious benefit from it." Rix's study of Japanese aid finds that "while indirect benefits to some segments of society (such as exporters) may be considerable, the primary reason for the existence of an aid policy lies outside the donor country and direct beneficiaries cannot normally participate in the public process."[23]

Rix emphasizes the role of the bureaucrats rather than big business. He argues that aid policy is "not the child of political pressures, elite decision-making or development arguments" but that "bureaucratic interests were the main determinants of the articulation of Japan's aid and economic cooperation policies."[24] For Rix this explains why aid policy lacks innovation, initiative, coordination, flexibility, and speed in formulation. In the case of strategic aid, however, the prime minister seems to have a significant role in the formulation of policy, thus rendering the bureaucratic politics model an incomplete framework for explaining the sudden rise of strategic aid policy.

Some analysts—mostly Japanese—have paid attention to the existence and occasional importance of political and security-related motives for aid. They provide that second dimension of aid and explain the regional concentration on Asia in political terms: Aid policy in Japan, including war reparations, was a child of the cold war and American policy in Asia. The cabinet of Yoshida Shigeru considered aid a cooperative venture with the United States and concentrated on Southeast Asia. Each successive cabinet followed this course by extending ODA to anticommunist or neutral countries in the region.[25] Japanese policy lacked a clear-cut, indigenous rationale from the very beginning; it merely followed in America's footsteps.[26]

Nishihara believes Japanese political interests in Southeast Asia commenced during the Ikeda Hayato period (1960–1964) with the attempted mediation of the Indonesia-Malaya dispute.[27] Japanese aid policy peaked at a turning point in the mid-1960s, according to many observers, especially in the wake of the U.S. bombing of North Vietnam following the Gulf of Tonkin incident. As the Vietnam War escalated, critics charge, the Japanese government increased grants and loans to Indonesia, Taiwan, Malaysia, Thailand, and especially to those nations supported by U.S. military activities: South Vietnam, Laos, and Cambodia.[28] Tokyo also normalized relations with South Korea in 1965, subsequently extending $500 million in aid, and joined the Asian and Pacific Council (ASPAC), a politically tinged regional organization founded in 1966 by Korean initiatives.[29] In other words critics charge that Japan followed the dictates of the United States, becoming embroiled indirectly in the Vietnam War through the use of economic aid.

The strength of the political argument is the inclusion of the underlying political and strategic criteria in analyzing the Japanese aid policy. It identifies a Japanese commitment to aid that flows beyond purely economic interests and provides a noneconomic explanation for aid concentration in Asia. But this view of political aid in the 1960s serves as a poor guide for analyzing strategic aid today. It is weak in explaining the globalization of aid policy. It pictures Japan as almost totally reactive, extending aid for reasons and to recipients determined by an outside force; it allows few indigenous political interests independent of the United States. It links Japanese aid policy to U.S. security interests and policy but fails to explain the direct relationship between aid and Japan's security policy. And most of these observers would continue to emphasize the primacy of economic motives for giving aid.

Japanese government officials present the emergence of political aid as a 1980s' phenomenon, a culmination of a natural evolutionary process. As a Foreign Ministry Official explains,

> In the 1960s, the main motives for Japan's economic cooperation were to promote its exports and assist its industries in overseas investment. . . . Promoting commercial and industrial interests was the main purpose of such cooperation. . . . In the 1970s especially after the oil crisis, the role of economic assistance as a means of securing raw materials such as oil came to be stressed. In other words, the reinforcement of economic interdependence became the main objective. . . . In the 1980s . . . the political and security sides of the objectives of economic cooperation are starting to receive greater emphasis.[30]

Two American aid analysts, Brooks and Orr, concur, using their own chronology of four overlapping phases in the evolution of Japan's aid policy: reparations from the mid-1950s to 1965; "excessively tied aid used primarily as a means to promote exports" from the mid-1950s to the early 1970s; "concentration of aid ... on resource-rich countries and countries along shipping routes in order to achieve economic interdependence" in the 1970s; and an emphasis on basic human needs, the poorest nations and "sensitivity to the humanitarian needs of countries of strategic importance" since the late 1970s.[31]

Brooks and Orr argue that Japan converted economic aid into a major political diplomatic tool because

> Tokyo was convinced that it had to devise a strategem to counter growing instability in key developing countries brought on by internal or external forces. Lacking a military or security assistance option because of its peace constitution, Tokyo realized that its means of influencing the course of world politics was limited almost entirely to economic and diplomatic tools.[32]

This political interpretation of aid policy's evolution can explain the increase in amounts and the expansion of aid beyond Asia to strategically important countries in the Middle East, Africa, and Latin America. It does not deny the large shadow cast by the United States or the Western alliance, but it stresses voluntarism on the part of the Japanese government. This view stresses shared, rather than subordinate, interests between Japan and its allies. Japan utilizes its national strengths—economic and financial resources—in an effort to share the security burden.

There is a danger, however, in accepting the Japanese government's pronouncements on globalization and politicization at face value. Globalization, while eye-catching, has been limited and halting. The rationale for political and strategic aid, while significant, has been confusing and inconsistently applied. Yet some observers imply that the political and strategic criteria now supercede the economic rationale for aid-giving: "There is still a commercial component in some current aid programs, but such examples are now the exception rather than the rule."[33] This conclusion is open to debate, but it does symbolize the growing recognition of and interest in the political-strategic dimension of Japan's economic aid policy.

Japan in Perspective

The problem of coming to grips with recent Japanese aid policy developments is compounded by the complex nature of economic assistance itself.

The phenomenon of foreign aid has proven an enigma to both analysts and practitioners. "Of the seeming and real innovations which the modern age has introduced into the practice of foreign policy," Morgenthau noted over two decades ago, "none has proved more baffling to both understanding and action than foreign aid."[34] Nation-states have long provided assistance to other countries in the form of tribute, subsidies, bribes, and military assistance, but foreign aid in its current form and scale is new: "The use of public funds for the specific purpose of promoting and assisting the economic development of other sovereign countries has no significant precedent before the Marshall Plan, and its present place as an element in the relations between advanced and underdeveloped parts of the world is first and foremost a consequence of the profound change in those relations after World War II."[35] According to another view, "What is new is the scale of foreign aid, its integration into the foreign policies of many states, and its conspicuous role in international relations. ... Only in recent years has it really become 'the new statecraft,' of sufficient scope and importance to justify special consideration and analysis."[36]

Special consideration and analysis have resulted in "the emergence of a new discipline of knowledge and a new profession of specialists," some analysts argue.[37] They assert that aid is now a distinct field of study that has even produced its own textbooks.[38] But despite voluminous studies of the aid phenomenon, "there is still much uncertainty about the whole foreign aid experience, including its essential rationale, its objectives, its relationship to economic growth, social change, and political development, and its impact on national policies and international relations.[39] Coherent, comprehensive theories of the aid phenomenon have yet to emerge. White suggests one reason: "Aid-users, unsurprisingly, are not very interested in theories about themselves, or about why they pursue some objectives in preference to others. They are interested in theories which will help them to devise strategies by which their objectives may be obtained."[40] Others cite the lack of attention to the study of international political economy.[41]

The lack of a standard, accepted aid theory heightens the attractiveness of other donors' experiences as models to apply to Japanese aid policy. Aid literature overwhelmingly centers on the United States, but the American model appears inappropriate for Japan's policy. The American aid style, practice, experience, and motives seem unique, unsuitable as a model for any nation. "Foreign aid policy, as conceived and initiated by the United States is something new under the sun," according to Waltz. "Since the war as never before, aid policies have been designed to deal with entire regions, indeed with major portions of the globe, without the expectation of direct returns to the donor, either military or economic, but with the much grander hope of changing national capabilities permanently and transforming whole societies and political systems."[42] Pye observes that "economic aid and technical assistance are essentially American innovations in the realm of foreign affairs ... [that] reflects accurately the peculiar genius of the American people, for it combines an opportunity for expressing idealism and generosity with an eminently practical device for advancing our enlightened self-interest."[43] Montgomery agrees that the impetus for aid is rooted deep within the American character: "Americans have never been satisfied to let things alone. One of our persistent—and least charming—qualities has been the national desire to tinker with the world."[44] And as Packenham makes clear, "special conditions," historical and sociocultural, gave rise to certain beliefs about economic and political development that have shaped U.S. aid policy in the postwar period. These assumptions are that "change and development are easy"; "all good things go together"; "radicalism and revolution are bad"; and "distributing power is more important than accumulating power."[45]

America's aid policy, born in the budding days of the cold war and nurtured through the nation's transformation into a superpower, consistently maintained a global strategic focus. This, according to several observers, constitutes the uniqueness of U.S. aid policy:

> Foreign aid is more than an extension of the American presence or payment for international favors: it is a strategic reflection of a world outlook. ... The distinctive characteristic of American aid is its strategic use in assisting other nations to attain economic, military, political, and social conditions that will contribute to a world order conceived to serve the ultimate interests of the free world.[46]

American aid policy subordinates economic interests to political-strategic considerations. According to Packenham, economic and technical assistance "contributed to economic development; and economic development in turn was seen as contributing to political development" (which he defined in terms of promoting democracy, stability, anticommunism, peace, world community, and pro-Americanism).[47] "The basic long-range goal of foreign aid is politicial," notes another analyst. "It is not economic development per se."[48] Nelson, observing that strategic and development aid use the same instruments (technical, capital, and commodity assistance), links economic and security aspects: "Major security programs and development programs can be viewed as a progression, moving from contained threat to aided growth to self-sustaining growth."[49] In the policy formulation process, however, the economic interest "almost never dominates specific aid decisions" and is only one of many considerations.[50] Kaplan argues that "the neglect of economic interests was intentional because they are, in fact minimal. ... No conceivable set of incentives can alter these facts—that the domestic U.S. market and the economies of other developed nations provide far more fertile ground for cultivation than do countries needing large aid programs. The nation's gains from aid . . . are not economic in nature, nor are such benefits likely to become significant for decades to come."[51]

The differences between U.S. and Japanese aid outlooks and approaches appear striking. The uniqueness of the American aid experience is accentuated by a glance at the experience of European donors. In terms of aid distribution patterns, few donors follow the global approach. For European nations, former colonial or other ties laid the basis for the donor-recipient relationship. Britain emphasizes the Commonwealth nations; France sends the overwhelming majority of its aid to French-speaking Africa; West Germany provides over half of its aid to only seven countries which are not in any geographic region; Belgium concentrates on Zaire; Italy prefers Somalia, Yugoslavia, and Ethiopia.[52] Japan's concentration on Asian nations seems natural in this light.

Nor do other aid-givers consistently accept the security priority of the United States. "The Cold War could and did act as a major stimulus for some donors, some of the time," observed one aid expert, but "it could not be an effective stimulus to all donors, all the time especially when the principal forum for the discussion of aid (DAC) was a specially created body, in which to talk about aid too openly in Cold War terms was regarded as slightly disreputable."[53] The West Germans, for example, have found that "security and long-term diplomatic strategy . . . have been of little effective significance" for aid policy and that "strictly commercial relations, especially private investment, constitute a superior mode of assistance."[54] Many Japanese remain acutely conscious of the important role played by the Third World in Japan's economic policy and in upholding the international economic system.

The Europeans and Japanese were also latecomers to the postwar aid game. They emerged from World War II as aid recipients, through such programs as the Marshall Plan and the U.S. occupation of Japan. Ohlin observes that "the concept of 'foreign aid to developing nations' had virtually no place in these countries, except as it referred to multilateral aid, until the late 1950s."[55] Cunningham maintains that German aid programs emerged as a response to U.S. pressure. Bonn's Ministry for Economic Cooperation was established in 1961 apparently as a "gesture towards the United States which had been pressing West Germany to go into the aid business in order to share its aid and defence burden."[56] Japan is not the only country accused of lacking an indigenous rationale for aid policy.

Although Japanese and European aid patterns and motives share some characteristics, comparisons are difficult. Smaller European nations stress multilateral aid more than Japan. Japan and Germany may share the concern over economic benefits, but Bonn lacks Japan's geographic concentration in a specific region. Japan and France share a decentralized aid decision-making system, but France's cultural and institutional ties with African nations are not duplicated in Japan's relations with its Asian neighbors. Nor are Japan-Asia ties structured along the lines of the British relationship with the Commonwealth. Although the use of Europe as a model for Japan's policy is difficult, the similarities should alert the observer to the possibility that the evolution of Japan's postwar aid policy is not a totally unusual and isolated phenomenon. It is the U.S. experience that is unique.

The search for the roots of Japan's strategic aid entails, as in the case of American aid policy, the pinpointing of the unique or special conditions that gave birth to economic aid policy's doctrines, assumptions, and rationale. The problem, however, is that, unlike the U.S., the Japanese government never clearly acknowledged or articulated a security rationale for aid prior to the 1980s. Economism ruled the day, and officials denied or muted strategic objectives. Japan lacked an official aid philosophy until 1980. This resulted in a strong impression that the strategic rationale sprang forth suddenly, like Athena from the brow of Zeus, in the 1980s. But special conditions did exist prior to the 1980s, and an understanding of these conditions is necessary in order to explain how a component of foreign economic policy became a pillar of overall foreign policy.

For the Japanese today, economic assistance policy reflects the strong desire to play a more active role in international affairs. The new assertiveness portends a weakening of Japan's reputation as a passive, silent power, an economic giant and political dwarf. Aid policy offers a unique vision of Japan as an "aid great power," a nation that contributes to world peace and stability through a peace diplomacy that eschews military might in favor of the utilization of economic and financial might. Aid policy then becomes the response of the second largest economy in the free world to external pressures to "do more" in world affairs and to national aspirations to do more as a nonmilitary power. Aid policy offers a middle course between a concerted and unwanted military buildup and continued military weakness; it involves the nation in East-West issues but through a North-South prism. But while popular support for economic assistance remains steady, strategic aid conjures up a slightly different and less popular vision, one that seemingly separates economic aid policy from the nonmilitary peace diplomacy and weds it to military defense policy. The security connotation of strategic aid causes unease among the people and the national leaders.

The leadership, in order to preserve the domestic consensus on aid, therefore attempts to dilute the strategic coloring of aid by utilizing the more popular rationales of humanitarianism and economic interdependence. But the result is the failure of the concept of strategic aid to define clearly the exact relationship between aid and defense policy. The cost of ambiguity has not only been conceptual confusion and incoherencies but also some confusion in policy implementation. Why, for example, should Japan extend substantial strategic aid to far off Turkey, where Tokyo has few economic and direct security interests, and hesitate on South Korea, a neighbor of great economic and strategic importance?

Since its debut in the late 1970s, strategic aid remains a policy in search of a rationale. But the irony is that despite growing pains, this very ambiguity in conceptualization and policy implementation allowed strategic aid to survive and flourish in a hesitant and often hostile domestic political environment. A clear-cut, unequivocal identification with defense policy would have sounded strategic aid's deathknell at birth. Strategic aid has come to represent a compromise between doing something and doing nothing in security and foreign policy. Therein lie both the strength and weakness of strategic assistance as concept and as policy.

Notes

1. See "Japan's Budget: Leadership and Control," *JEI Report* (February 17, 1984).
2. "Japan's Defense: Perceptions and Realities," ibid., February 10, 1984, and *Asahi Shimbun*, January 3, 1985.
3. Bruce Roscoe, "An Argument over Aid—And What It Really Amounts To," *Far Eastern Economic Review*, June 13, 1985, p. 86.
4. *New York Times*, September 30, 1981; Robert Lubar, "Reaganizing the Third World," *Fortune*, November 16, 1981, pp. 80–90; John Fenton, "U.S. Role in the World Bank Faces New Tests," *Congressional Quarterly Weekly Review*, February 27, 1982, pp. 451–6; and U.S. Department of the Treasury, *United States Participation in the Multilateral Development Banks in the 1980s* (Washington, D.C.: U.S. Goverment Printing Office, 1982).
5. Teiichi Yamamoto, "White Paper: 'Present Status and Prospects for Economic Cooperation,'" *Look Japan*, March 10, 1983, p. 18.
6. See Japan, Ministry of Foreign Affairs, Economic Cooperation Bureau, "Japan's Economic Cooperation, "Japan's Economic Cooperation," February 1, 1982 (mimeographed handbook).
7. *Asahi Shimbun*, January 3, 1985.
8. For Japan's relations with the Asian Development Bank, see Dennis T. Yasutomo, *Japan and the Asian Development Bank* (New York: Praeger Special Studies, 1983).
9. See *Yomiuri Shimbun*, July 21, 1985, and *Japan Times Weekly*, August 10, 1985, October 5, 1985, and October 19, 1985.
10. Japan, Ministry of Foreign Affairs, *Japan's Official Development Assistance 1984 Annual Report* (1985), p. 24. See also, Shigekazu Matsumoto, "Progress and Policy Formulations of Japan's External Assistance," paper delivered at "The U.S. Congress and the Japanese Diet: Conference on Comparative Studies in Foreign Policy," Honolulu, February 9–12, 1983, p. 22.
11. Yasukichi Yasuba, "Economic Assistance Policy Needs Overhaul," *Look Japan*, April 10, 1982, p. 28.

12. Interview with a Ministry of Foreign Affairs official, February 16, 1983.

13. See Comprehensive National Security Study Group, *Report on Comprehensive National Security* (Tokyo: Prime Minister's Office, 1980).

14. Japan, Ministry of Foreign Affairs, *Diplomatic Bluebook, 1981 Edition: Review of Recent Developments in Japan's Foreign Relations* (Tokyo: Foreign Press Center/Japan, 1981), p. 30.

15. Terutomo Ozawa, *Multinationalism, Japanese Style* (Princeton, N.J.: Princeton University Press, 1979), pp. 34-5.

16. Shinsuke Samejima, "Can Japan Steer Its Foreign Aid Policy Clear of Militarism?" *Japan Quarterly* (January-March 1982): 36.

17. John White, *Japanese Aid* (London: Overseas Development Institute, 1964).

18. Alexander J. Caldwell, "The Evolution of Japanese Economic Cooperation, 1950-1970," in Harald B. Malmgren, ed., *Pacific Basin Development: The American Interests* (Lexington, Mass. Lexington Books, 1972), pp. 61-80; and Ken Matsui, *Keizai Kyoryoku; Towareru Nihon no Keizai Gaiko* (Tokyo: Yuhikaku, 1983).

19. Martha F. Loutfi, *The Net Cost of Japanese Foreign Aid* (New York: Praeger, 1973), p. 48.

20. Sukehiro Hasegawa, *Japanese Foreign Aid: Policy and Practice* (New York: Praeger, 1975).

21. Alan Rix, *Japan's Economic Aid* (New York: St. Martin's Press, 1980), p. 11.

22. Ken Matsui, *Keizai Kyoryoku*, pp. 151-7.

23. John White, *The Politics of Foreign Aid* (New York: St. Martin's Press, 1964), p. 50; and Rix, *Japan's Economic Aid*, p. 84.

24. Rix, ibid., p. 267.

25. Yuji Suzuki, "Gunkaku to Fukyo no Naka no Keizai Kyoryoku," *Sekai*, July 1983, pp. 53-4; and Matsumoto, "Progress and Policy," pp. 2-3.

26. Toshio Shishido, *Tonan Ajia Enjo o Kangaeru* (Tokyo: Toyo Keizai Shimposha, 1973), pp. 30-1.

27. Masashi Nishihara, *The Japanese and Sukarno's Indonesia: Tokyo-Jakarta Relations, 1951-1966* (Honolulu: University of Hawaii Press, 1976), p. 8.

28. Hidetoshi Taga, "Sengo Nihon no Keizai Enjo no Kiseki," *Ajia*, (May 1982): 88-9; Tsuyoshi Yamamoto, *Nihon no Keizai Enjo* (Tokyo: Sanseido, 1978), pp. 72-83; and Matsumoto, "Progress and Policy," p. 5.

29. Yamamoto, ibid., pp. 84-5.

30. Koichiro Matsuura, "Japan's Role in International Cooperation," *National Development* (September 1981):64-5.

31. William L. Brooks and Robert M. Orr, Jr., "Japan's Foreign Economic Assistance," *Asian Survey* 25(March 1985):323.

32. Ibid.

33. Ibid., p. 339.

34. From the forward to George Liska, *The New Statecraft; Foreign Aid in American Foreign Policy* (Chicago: University of Chicago Press, 1960), p. vii.

35. Goran Ohlin, *Foreign Aid Policies Reconsidered* (Paris: OECD, 1966), p. 9.

36. Norman D. Palmer, "Foreign Aid and Foreign Policy: The 'New Statecraft' Reassessed," *Orbis* (Fall 1969):764.

37. Ohlin, *Policies Reconsidered*, p. 9.

38. R. D. McKinlay and R. Little, "A Foreign Policy Model of U.S. Bilateral Aid Allocation," *World Politics* (October 1977):58, fn. 2.

39. Palmer, "Foreign Aid," p. 781-2.

40. White, *Politics*, p. 106.

41. McKinlay and Little maintain that

> though economists have widely recognized the foreign policy context of aid, they have considered an examination of this aspect of aid to be outside their sphere of competence. Political developmentalists have focused mainly on the domestic political structures of low-income countries and have to a large extent ignored the external setting of these countries. .... Foreign policy analysts have been preoccupied with classifying foreign policy behavior and have tended to ignore the political aspects of economic behavior.

See "Foreign Policy Model," pp. 61, fn. 8.

42. Kenneth N. Waltz, *Foreign Policy and Democratic Politics* (Boston: Little, Brown, 1967), p. 185.

43. Lucien W. Pye, "Soviet and American Styles in Foreign Aid," *Orbis* (Summer 1960):159.

44. John D. Montgomery, *Foreign Aid in International Politics* (Englewood Cliffs, N.J.: Prentice-Hall, 1967), p. 2. Liska traces American foreign aid roots to the federal grants-in-aid program, in *New Statecraft*, p. 24.

45. Robert A. Packenham, *Liberal America and the Third World* (Princeton, N.J.: Princeton University Press, 1973), pp. 19-20.

46. Montgomery, *Foreign Aid*, pp. 18 and 23.

47. Packenham, *Liberal America*, p. 4.

48. Lloyd D. Black, *The Strategy of Foreign Aid* (Princeton, N.J.: D. Van Nostrand, 1968), p. 18.

49. Joan M. Nelson, *Aid, Influence, and Foreign Policy* (New York: Macmillan, 1968), p. 18.

50. Ibid., p. 111.

51. Jacob J. Kaplan, *The Challenge of Foreign Aid* (New York: Praeger, 1967), pp. 163-4. Kaplan also argues that "the very meagerness of material recompense explains much of the weakness of Congressional support for aid programs." Kaplan wrote his book before the onset of the oil and debt crises.

52. See George Cunningham, *The Management of Aid Agencies* (London: Croom Helm, 1974).

53. White, *Politics*, p. 22.

54. Ohlin, *Policies Reconsidered*, p. 41.

55. Ibid., p. 26.

56. Cunningham, *Managment*, p. 134.

2
Strategic Aid as Concept

> Japan should be in a position to undertake a series of coordinated measures—economic, diplomatic, and military—aimed at the avoidance of armed conflict. The "economic diplomacy" pursued by a succession of Japanese premiers is one potential instrument for the avoidance of war.
>
> —Momoi Makoto

> Aid can't stop a tank.
>
> —A Japanese Defense Expert

A little over a half century ago, Japanese armed forces began sweeping across the mainland and sea-lanes of the Asia Pacific region. By the end of 1945, however, the Japanese nation lay prostrate, faced with the enormous task of rebuilding a shattered economy, society, and pride under foreign rule. The lesson of the prewar years seemed clear: The military path to peace and prosperity had failed.

Japan, ruled by a samurai class and shaped by a warrior ethic, sustained a militaristic tradition throughout much of its history. The society developed in isolation, relatively free from serious foreign threats. Japan had never experienced a successful military invasion or foreign occupation, nor a defeat in war, until 1945. Japan developed as a culture and society with a strong identity, as a unique people and nation. The populace lived on a clearly defined territorial unit, as an island country, and developed a homogeneous society imbued with a strong "we–they," "us–them" attitude toward the outside world.

Militarism and nationalism served as the foundation for Japanese modernization and imperialism in the late nineteenth and early twentieth centuries. They were the two driving forces that propelled Japan onto the world stage as a great power and eventually led to Pearl Harbor. But World War II transformed the nation. The Japanese in the postwar period perceived militarism as a tradition that failed, a tradition that had betrayed the people and brought defeat, suffering, and humiliation. Almost overnight a deep revulsion developed against anything associated with the military or militarism. A strong pacifist consciousness blossomed in place of militarism, and pacifism became an emotional force that shaped much of postwar Japanese politics.

World War II also discredited nationalism, at least the old style, jingoistic nationalism. The Japanese today prefer the word adopted from English for nationalism, *nashionarizumu,* almost as if the concept were now foreign to Japanese culture. "Patriotism" is a term almost never heard. The spirit of nationalism did not die, however, but was transformed. Economism has replaced the emperor and the state as the focal point of the nationalistic spirit. National pride today is measured not by military strength but by economic strength, prowess, and accomplishments.

These developments have greatly affected postwar foreign policy. Japanese diplomacy focused decidedly and almost exclusively on economic relations with other nations. This economic diplomacy consciously separated economic aspects from political and strategic matters, thereby satisfying the aspirations of a pacifist society for a "peace diplomacy." Japan avoided extensive political entanglements that might lead the nation into unwanted—and someone else's—conflicts. The restrictions on the use of force stipulated in Article Nine of the Constitution accurately reflected the general sentiments of the people:

> Aspiring sincerely to an international peace based on justice and order, the Japanese people forever renounce war as a sovereign right of the nation and the threat or use of force as means of settling international disputes.
>
> In order to accomplish the aim of the preceding paragraph, land, sea, and air forces, as well as other war potential, will never be maintained. The right of belligerency of the state will not be recognized.

As for defense policy, the Japanese stressed self-defense, which successive cabinets defined as a limited, minimal military buildup and role designed to secure the safety of the home islands in case of external aggression or internal subversion. They coupled this "exclusively defensive defense" policy with heavy reliance on conventional and nuclear capability of the United States under the provisions of the U.S.-Japan Security Treaty. The Japanese considered the concentration on economic development at home, economic relations abroad, and a minimal, purely defensive security role as the antidote for the mistakes of the era that culminated in World War II.

The results are well known. Japan has become a prosperous nation, and its people have enjoyed peace for four decades without the loss of a single life in combat. This outcome affirms, in Japanese minds, the basic correctness of the concentration on economic accomplishments and justifies the cautious attitude toward military security policy. GNP statistics of the late 1960s seemed to reflect accurately the postwar national priorities and aspirations: an annual average growth rate of over 10 percent and defense spending totaling less than 1 percent of GNP.

A Turning Point

Something happened during the 1970s. Japan had achieved its postwar goals: reconstruction, economic growth, prosperity, and peace. The nation had fulfilled its self-devised historic mission to catch up with the West. In many ways Japan surpassed most Western nations by achieving the status of second largest economy in the free world. Japan had gained widespread recognition, admiration, and respect for its economic miracle. But along the way Tokyo also earned international envy and resentment for those very same economic accomplishments, especially among its major trading partners. Trade friction erupted in the 1970s, coupled with American charges that Japan enjoyed a "free ride" on the backs of American taxpayers for its defense.

Many Japanese have come to regard Western criticism as scapegoating, an effort by Americans and Europeans to mask their own economic short-comings and failure to put their own houses in order. Japan, they fear, is being penalized for its success. Nevertheless, the government has moved to mitigate these tensions in the interest of maintaining smooth relations with friends. These efforts to soften the rough spots in trade and defense relations coincide with a growing conviction in Japan that the nation needs new national goals to replace those that had guided the people through the first three and a half decades of the postwar period.

In the 1980s one candidate for a new national goal is "internationaliza-tion." A conviction has taken hold that Japan's major mission in the world should be international service. Japan's new status allows and demands greater contributions to international society economically, politically, and securitywise. The contents of the internationalization slogan are ill defined. It is a popular catchphrase that can include everything from opening domes-tic markets to studying foreign languages and cultures. In foreign policy, it connotes a rejection of the traditional isolationist attitudes of the past, an escape from the island country mentality, and a commitment to an active and involved, rather than a passive and reactive, approach to international relations. In the words of one observer, a "new assertiveness" has arisen: "The feeling that Japan should do something in international affairs more than doggedly pursue its own economic self-interest has become widespread. But agreement about what the 'something' should be has yet to be forged."[1]

Momentous developments in the international environment spurred the search for that something but did not make it any easier to forge an agreement. Japan felt the reverberations from the declaration of the Nixon Doctrine, the collapse of the Bretton Woods international economic system, two oil crises, a Sino-American rapprochement, a continued Soviet military buildup in the Asia Pacific region, the fall of Saigon and subsequent withdrawal of American troops from the Southeast Asian mainland, the Soviet invasion of Afghanistan, the Vietnamese incursion into Kampuchea, Sino-Vietnamese border clashes, the Iranian hostage crisis, the onset of greater tension in the oil-rich Persian Gulf region, and the rise and demise of Soviet-American détente. On top of it all, Japan's perplexing friction with the United States on trade and defense issues intensified and escalated as the decade of the 1970s drew to a close.

One consequence of these developments was the advent of a defense debate and a closer examination of national security needs and capabilities. Closer consideration, however, should not be equated with a return to the military path to national defense despite an ever-threatening external environment:

> One should not exaggerate the degree of movement toward a more forthcoming defense posture or underestimate the domestic opposition to major departures in Japan's defense policy. . . . There is not much evidence that Japan can be prepared to do considerably more in expanding its defense capabilities than it currently plans to do, or that the deterioration in the international security environment that was both symbolized and furthered by the invasion of Afghanistan will shock Japan into doing more.[2]

The military path remains highly unpopular, giving the impression that "military defense played little or no part in their [Japanese] own thinking, the keys to their security being found primarily in the skills of their diplomacy, the vigor of their economy, the strength of their political system and the health of their public morale."[3] The reason, according to one Japanese defense specialist, is that

> The Japanese public is broadly skeptical about the utility of military power as a means of assuring national security. Most Japanese believe that military power in itself does not symbolize either national prestige or glory. Nor do they see it as effectively serving political or economic purposes, as was assumed to be the case prior to World War II. . . . The problem is that the Japanese public tends to dismiss military power altogether as a means of helping to maintain national security.[4]

The result has been a situation where

> caution, a risk-minimization orientation to international political affairs, and a conviction that more costs than benefits would result from a major military role that would move beyond a limited conception of conventional self-defense remain keynotes of Japanese foreign policy.[5]

If the military option remains unpopular among the people, then how should Japan pursue national security? "In the final analysis," writes a

Japanese aid expert, "a security strategy should not be carried out through military power but should be exercised by using economic strength as power."[6] The view that an economic giant should contribute to international society through economic means maintains strong appeal in Japan. While trade and direct investment flows indicate primarily private efforts in the international arena, Official Development Assistance symbolizes official commitment. Aid is a visible measure for Japanese participation in international circles. More important, it is a nonmilitary yardstick, and the Japanese people tend to think of aid in terms of amounts rather than rationales: "Japan's aid first took the form of reparations for damages inflicted during the war and created a strong feeling that aid meant only providing money."[7]

What, in theory, can providing money accomplish politically and strategically? Knorr discusses six short-term expected political and military "payoffs":

1. "To compete for political influence . . . against rival states" and also "to gain or keep military allies or to disrupt antagonistic alliances"

2. To maintain friendly relations with other nations

3. To support a politically or militarily valuable government that is subject to economic, domestic, or foreign pressure

4. "To preserve the military security of the donor state"

5. To enhance the image of a donor state by demonstrating concern about world poverty

6. "To signal to third countries a political commitment to a recipient country"[8]

In this and the following chapter, one will note that the Japanese government is comfortable with all of these expected short-term payoffs. Each cabinet emphasizes especially points 2, 5, and 6. They correspond to three underlying inclinations of Japanese diplomacy: to maintain friendly relations with all nations, to enhance national prestige (in this case by contributing to the solution of the North-South problem), and to demonstrate that Japan is a loyal ally by aiding recipient nations important to Western security interests. The government would hesitate to acknowledge openly the blatant politically manipulative implications and intentions of point 1, and it has softened the direct linkage between aid and security stipulated in point 4 for domestic political reasons.

Knorr also delineates long-term political and strategic payoffs, including the assumption that recipient nations will be able to withstand external aggression more effectively as the economy develops and the government stabilizes. In addition, "as poor countries become economically better off, their behavior will become less disruptive and cantankerous, and more stable and peaceful." Finally, "the economic growth of the destitute countries is also expected to produce a more congenial world environment in terms of institutions and policies," by which Knorr means these nations will become more pluralistic, democratic, and free-market oriented.[9] These long-term assumptions succinctly conform to Japanese thinking on the strategic uses of economic aid.

Janus

Japanese aid proponents have recently begun to articulate two strands of thought. Some view economic aid as a substitute for military security efforts, while others view it as supplementary. The starting point for both schools is the premise, as stated by Prime Minister Suzuki Zenko, that "Under our Constitution based on peace, Japanese defense is dedicated to purely defensive capabilities. We will not become a military power threatening neighboring countries, and we have as our basic policy a firm commitment to the three nonnuclear principles."[10]

The former view envisions aid policy as Japan's distinctive contribution to international affairs as an economic great power. The *Asahi Shimbun* advocates this approach: "While continuing its efforts to ease international tension, Japan should cut the increase in defense expenditures and take the lead in helping the debt-ridden developing countries."[11] Since the people want to preserve the peace Constitution, why not become an "aid superpower," allocating 1 percent of GNP to aid (roughly equivalent to defense spending) and providing 40 percent of all of the donor nations' ODA to the Third World? Japan's international influence as an "aid superpower," the *Asahi* concludes, can then become a source of national pride and its raison d'être as a nation-state.[12]

A group of economic officials in the Economic Planning Agency, writing in private capacities, notes Japan's epoch-making potential to become an economic power without substantial military might. Japan's aid gains in importance, they note, as U.S. and West German aid decreases. Japan can become an "aid great power." What is an aid great power? This group's definition includes "thinking big," for example contributing to the building of a second Panama Canal, and a momentous increase in aid amounts: 3 to 5 percent of GNP, with 1 percent for defense expenditures and 2 percent for economic cooperation.[13]

Those who consider aid a supplementary means of enhancing national security take a more pragmatic and less grandiose view. A Foreign Ministry official views aid as one, and not the only, link in the security chain:

If we are to refrain from becoming a great military power in fulfilling our increased responsibilities in the field of international politics, it must be economic power that Japan relies upon as a tool to back up its position in playing its role. Economic cooperation can be conceived as one of the important elements of "comprehensive security."[14]

The basic assumption of these aid proponents is the strong belief that Japan must contribute to international society in the political and strategic as well as economic arenas. They do not advocate the avoidance of these responsibilities, but they feel that Japan's defense capabilities are limited constitutionally, politically, and psychologically. Foreign aid must, therefore, help fill the gap in defense capability. In the words of a former Foreign Minister, "The need for a serious Japanese commitment to foreign aid is underscored by the low level of our nation's defense expenditures. The heavy burden imposed by defense costs makes it difficult for the U.S. and Western European nations to provide very much foreign aid. It is all the more important that Japan step in and use some of its economic resources to benefit the world."[15] According to a Liberal Democratic Party (LDP) member, "Aid must be considered from the standpoint of national interest and not just humanitarian aspects. There should be more thought given to aid along strategic lines. At this point in time, Japanese military efforts are restricted, but aid is possible. To some extent, aid can be seen as a substitute for defense efforts, but Japan must view them [aid and military policy] equally."[16]

This sense of balance between aid and military efforts is prevalent among the advocates of aid as a supplement to defense policy. As Prime Minister Ohira Masayoshi put it, Japanese security "will be concretely realized, but not by military power alone but through the linked support of economic power, information, political power and diplomacy. It will not do if one link in the chain is too strong or too weak. My meaning is that they should be well-balanced."[17] This sense of balance is also evident in the recommendations of the Forum for Policy Innovation, a private think tank. The Forum recommended that 3 percent of the GNP be allocated for comprehensive security purposes, with food and energy policy, defense, and ODA receiving a share of 1 percent each. ODA would, as envisioned by the *Asahi Shimbun*, constitute 40 percent of total aid contributions of the member nations of the Development Assistance Committee (DAC) of the Organization for Economic Cooperation and Development (OECD).[18]

Both of these approaches support the uses of economic aid as a diplomatic tool, but they differ on objectives and rationale. The latter view, which prefers a national interest tinge for aid policy, is encompassed in the concept of comprehensive national security. One would expect, therefore, that comprehensive security would provide a clear explanation of the aid-security link. The concept, however, confronts the observer with a *Rashomon*-like dilemma of determining the true nature of aid's role in Japanese security policy. For aid reveals its Janus-like quality because comprehensive security as a concept actually accommodates both of these visions of economic aid.

Comprehensive National Security

Official interest in comprehensive security emerged during the cabinet of Ohira Masayoshi (1978–1980). The Ohira cabinet bore the brunt of a series of disturbing external crises, including the invasions of Afghanistan and Kampuchea, the Iranian hostage crisis, and a second oil shock. The government responded to each crisis with ad hoc policy measures, including economic sanctions and a boycott of the 1980 Olympics in Moscow, but realized that the traditional passive and reactive diplomatic posture no longer served the interests of the nation well.

The upheavals in the outside world triggered complex responses in Japan. On the one hand the Japanese perceived a steady erosion of U.S. military and economic power in the world. They perceived the gradual diminution of the world's banker and policeman and began to question the credibility of U.S. defense commitments to Japan. The corresponding Soviet military buildup in Asia and attainment of nuclear parity with the United States, coupled with the thinning of the ranks in the U.S. Seventh Fleet, seemed to symbolize a new power balance in the region. On the other hand the external crises reinforced the importance of outside help for Japan's security. The invasions of Kampuchea and Afghanistan greatly eroded the appeal and viability of autonomous defense, which was never strong or widespread to begin with. The Ohira cabinet responded by moving closer to its ally: "For both military and economic reasons, the tie with America seemed more important than ever, and the Treaty symbolized that tie."[19] But in addition, Ohira broadened Japan's security perspective to include Western Europe. Ohira began to speak more about Japan's place in the Western alliance system and not just its status as an ally of the United States. His successors echoed a major theme that emerged during his cabinet that Japan will contribute to international affairs as a loyal ally of the West.

Ohira's closer identification and cooperation with the Western alliance did not reflect an intention to increase massively Japan's defense spending. The prime minister favored the status quo, as did the majority of the populace. Rather, he defined "contributing" to the West within the framework of comprehensive national security, stressing its nonmilitary aspects. Ohira's reaction to international crises reflected an increasingly widespread recognition in Japan

> that threats to security were not limited to the politico-military field but were as likely, and in fact more likely, to occur in the economic field. Even without an armed attack on Japanese territory, life or property, security threats could arise as a result of local wars or events in which Japan was not directly involved. Consequently, the definition of a security threat came to include such eventualities as an interruption in the supply of raw materials, particularly oil, sudden price rises and food embargoes. Such threats can occur even in peace time.[20]

Some kind of strategy was, therefore, required to cope with nonmilitary threats in peacetime as well as military threats in times of emergency, especially when military self-defense faced domestic obstacles:

> According to Japan's Constitution, the maintenance of military might is forbidden, as everyone knows, but self-defense is an inherent right of a nation-state and Japan does have that right as a natural law that transcends the Constitution. Japan thus has the right of self-defense but does not possess military power ... [Therefore] when thinking about our nation's defense, it is natural to emphasize a wide range of security efforts that do not depend on the centrality of military security efforts.[21]

Ohira's search for nonmilitary security options led to his creation of the Study Group on Comprehensive National Security in April 1979. The group, composed of academics, businessmen, and government officials, examined military and nonmilitary aspects of security throughout the following year. It submitted its report on July 2, 1980 to Acting Prime Minister Ito Masayoshi, who temporarily filled the post following Ohira's untimely death in office.[22]

Suzuki Zenko enthusiastically embraced the report's findings upon taking office as prime minister in the summer of 1980, and in December, he adopted comprehensive national security as national policy. Suzuki singled out economic cooperation as a pillar of comprehensive national security, and government officials thereafter linked aid with the nonmilitary sector of national security policy.

The Ohira study group's *Report on Comprehensive National Security* set forth a series of moderate recommendations. One analyst refers to the *Report* as "perhaps the most succinct statement of the political realists' position," which focuses primarily on the political and diplomatic implications of security policy. Thus, "domestically, they are sensitive to the persistence of pacifist sentiments and fears that a major rearmament could lead again to the growth of the military's political power and ... they are concerned about the possible trade-off between economic welfare and military expenditures." They favor a strengthening of ties to the United States and argue for a more involved Japanese role in shouldering security burdens of the Western alliance. Political realists believe that defense improvements should focus on qualitative rather than quantitative expansion.[23]

Political realists do not consider the Soviet Union primarily a military threat: "They think the Soviets are more likely to exploit instability in the Third World for Soviet gains than to make direct military attacks on interests vital to the West." Their major concern is economic vulnerability, against which they propose countermeasures that include diversifying sources of raw materials, stockpiling and economic aid programs "to Third World nations which are not only critical raw material suppliers, but also strategically important countries from a military perspective."[24]

While Ohira's study group touched on economic assistance, its treatment of the relationship between aid and security is far from clear. It highlights aid's importance as a component of comprehensive security but does not attempt to integrate aid with other components. It views economic aid as primarily relevant to the North-South problem and fails to discuss implications in the East-West realm.

The *Report* places the onus on the developed nations for improving North-South relations and prescribes a special role for Japan: "Japan's world historic mission is to play a leading role in creating an order between the North and the South."[25] The stakes are high: If the North fails to respond to the needs of the South, trade relations would suffer and "xenophobic riots" may occur, a reference to the upheavals in the Ayatollah Khomeini's Iran. The Study Group even painted an apocalyptic picture of the consequences of a failure to help the South: "The ensuing confusion in international political and economic systems could even threaten the existence of all countries including the developing countries themselves."[26] Since critical natural resources flow to Japan from the developing world, Japan's interests demand active diplomacy toward the South.

The Study Group views aid as a practical diplomatic tool. The *Report* assumes that Japan's economic growth will continue to outpace other developed nations'. Japan will, therefore, possess the financial capability to become a premier aid-giving power. And it is in the realm of economic power that Japan can shine, especially because of the inadequacy of military power. But while the Study Group recommends that Japan's "application of economic cooperation must rest on comprehensive judgments that take into account political as well as economic considerations," it limits aid's use to nonmilitary support for a recipient nation: "Japan cannot exert influence on other nations with military power or build friendly relations by contributing to other nations' military security."[27]

The *Report* remains vague on the contents of "political consideration." Rather than discuss methods for using aid politically, determining the criteria for its use or methods of determining specific recipient countries, the idea of political considerations merits only that one sentence, and an observation in the following paragraph appears to contradict or at least cast doubt on the effectiveness of this approach: "Many countries are hopeful of assistance from Japan also because it is a reliable economic power that can be counted on to be free of political ambitions."[28] What would be the effect if Japan politicizes an aid policy that relies on its nonpolitical nature for its appeal in many recipient countries? The *Report* also fails to discuss situations where recipient nations would welcome overtly political aid from Japan.

The *Report's* treatment of the relationship between economic cooperation and security maintains its ambiguity. It postulates three stages or levels

Table 2-1
Comprehensive National Security Levels

Security policy in a narrow sense

First-level efforts: creation of a more peaceful international order
  International cooperation
  Cooperation with countries that may become enemies, through arms control and confidence-building measures

Second-level efforts: intermediary measures
  An alliance, or cooperation with countries sharing common political ideals and interests

Third-level efforts: self-reliant efforts
  Consolidation of denial capability, that is, capability to prevent the easy establishment of a fait accompli; at its base, fostering of denial capability of the state and society as a whole, strong will to protect the state's independent existence even by making sacrifices

Economic security policy

First-level efforts: management and maintenance of the independent order
  Maintenance of the free-trade system
  Resolution of the North–South problem

Second-level efforts: intermediary measures
  Promotion of friendly relations with a number of nations that are important to a nation's economy

Third-level efforts: self-reliant efforts
  Stockpiling
  A certain degree of self-sufficiency
  Basically, the maintenance of the nation's economic strength, that is, maintaining productivity and competitive export power

Source: Comprehensive National Security Study Group, *Report on Comprehensive National Security,* July 2, 1980, p. 21.

of response to military and nonmilitary threats. Stage 1 constitutes the prevention or elimination of threats through influencing the surrounding environment; stage 2 foresees certain intermediate measures, such as the promotion of friendly relations with nations important to Japan economically (which appears to be indistinguishable from stage one); and stage 3 concerns the management of actual threats on the basis of self-reliance, including military defense.[29] (See table 2-1.)

In this scheme one would assume that aid is viewed as the nation's first line of defense. As a component of stage 1 or 2, aid would assist in creating friendly relations with other nations and promote a more peaceful, interdependent world. Presumably, Japan would resort to drastic measures such as military defense only when the nonmilitary deterrent and effort fails. But even this is unclear since the table places these three levels under two other conceptual rubrics: "Security policy in a narrow sense," or military-related aspects, and "economic security policy." (The *Report* elsewhere refers to the existence of "other security forms" as well.) Theoretically, economic assistance can find a niche in the first and second levels of both "narrow" and "economic" security, but since the *Report* discusses aid only in terms of economic policy and the North-South problem, one must assume it applies only to the first level of the economic security side of the ledger.

However one interprets this *Report*, it seems fairly evident that economic aid and military security are separate and distinct components of security policy despite the "comprehensive" rubric. They seem related only indirectly, for the *Report* does not dwell on the integration of these two sectors. The *Report* did not attempt to mask its advocacy of improving military defense preparedness with a nonmilitary red herring. It proposed a qualitative improvement in "self-denial" capabilities and proposed a 20 percent per annum increase in defense spending, which would carry the defense budget over the 1 percent of GNP level.[30] As a Foreign Ministry official asserted to his colleagues at an intraministerial meeting, "No matter how one explains it, what cannot be forgotten is that comprehensive national security is a concept that includes military aspects as well as nonmilitary aspects." Comprehensive security does not mean substituting nonmilitary for military measures: "There is no trade-off relationship."[31]

The equal emphasis placed on both nonmilitary and military methods in theory created a "Take from it what you want" atmosphere surrounding discussions of comprehensive security. Comprehensive security thus satisfied few: "For some observers, the term appears as a smokescreen behind which the hawks can expand defence spending. . . . For others, it is claimed to involve a downgrading of the military security element and is held to mean exactly the opposite, i.e., reduction of military spending in favour of diplomatic and economic initiatives."[32] The murkiness of the concept shielded economic assistance from serious criticism because of its uncertain relationship with security policy. And aid-policymakers were not about to challenge the domestic consensus on economic cooperation policy when they formulated a Japanese aid philosophy.

Japan's Aid Philosophy

The Japanese government extended economic aid to developing nations without an aid philosophy for over two decades. A major study of Japan's aid policy published as late as 1980 could definitely declare that Japan lacked any philosophy in granting aid beyond economic motives.[33] As that book rolled off the presses, however, policymakers in Tokyo were toiling over the tenets that would constitute the nation's first formal aid philosophy.

The Ministry of Foreign Affairs (MFA) initiated a study of aid policy in spring 1980. By November, four months after the submission of the Ohira Study Group *Report*, the results were ready for unveiling. Within a period of a half year, Japan suddenly possessed a full-blown philosophy, published in

April 1981 as a booklet entitled *Keizai Kyoryoku no Rinen—Seifu Kaihatsu Enjo Wa Naze Okonau no ka* (The Philosophy of Economic Cooperation— Why Give Official Development Assistance?).[34]

The MFA's formulation of the new aid philosophy stresses humanitarian motives for extending assistance to the Third World and recognizes the importance of the interdependence rationale. Comprehensive security receives its own chapter, in which is found four reasons for extending aid under the comprehensive security rubric.[35]

1. Aid is a necessary "cost" if Japan is to remain a peaceful country *(heiwa kokka)*. The booklet notes Japan's negative attitude toward and lack of participation in international security efforts. It presents the need for a comprehensive view of security and argues for a less passive diplomacy. Aid, according to the publication, will help reduce tensions between the North and South and will therefore contribute to a stable world order.

2. Aid is a necessary "cost" if Japan is to remain an economic great power. The booklet highlights Japan's vulnerability to a deterioration in North-South relations. The private sector has taken the lead in economic relations with developing nations, it observes, but this has given rise to numerous problems; for example, recipient nations complain of Japanese "overpresence" or about the lack of mutual benefits when private firms are interested primarily in the pursuit of their own profits. The Japanese government, suggests the booklet, can step in to reduce tension through providing ODA that contributes to the welfare of the recipient nation's people.

3. Aid can strengthen weak spots in overseas economic dependence. Japan's dependence on overseas sources of raw materials and markets is higher than other industrialized nations. Many developing nations, moreover, are geographically located in strategic locations, and astride sea transport lanes. The book cites Indonesia, Malaysia, and Singapore as guardians of the Strait of Malacca, through which passes 85 percent of Japan's oil supply and 40 percent of its foreign trade. The friendship of these nations, stresses the booklet, is critical for Japan.

4. Japan can assist developing nations because of its status as a non-Western development model. The booklet assumes that Japan's history of modernization is attractive to developing nations because of its rapid industrialization within a century, its non-Western society and culture, and its lack of a colonial legacy in most of the Third World. It acknowledges Japanese actions in Asia during World War II, but it then notes that this imperialist experience did not extend to Africa, Latin America, or the Middle East. Japan as a result lacks political ambitions in these areas, according to the philosophy, and is thus in an advantageous position to gain the trust and

respect of the Third World. It even borrows the Ohira *Report's* phrase, "world historic mission," to refer to its role as a development model.

The new aid philosophy's handling of the relationship between aid and security remains vague and confusing. The Ohira *Report* was more forthcoming in its advocacy of political uses of aid, even though it lacked details on how this was to be done. The Foreign Ministry's philosophy stops short of openly advocating the use of aid to obtain specific strategic objectives. The thrust of its justification for economic aid is hard to distinguish from overall foreign economic policy goals, that is, promoting friendly relations with nations in order to secure resources and maintain markets to keep Japan an economic great power. The Ohira Study Group *Report* devoted only one sentence to the importance of resources and markets.

The MFA booklet cites the Ohira report's formulation of three levels or stages of security, but the philosophy exacerbates rather than clears the confusion. While the Ohira *Report* would place aid within level 1 and possibly level 2 (crisis prevention and intermediate measures), the MFA booklet maintains that aid is relevant to levels one and three. It views aid as a means of closing the North-South gap while establishing solidarity with countries sharing common ideals and interests, which are levels 1 and 2 in the Ohira *Report*.[36]

Even comprehensive security's relationship with economic assistance is obscure in the Foreign Ministry conceptualization. The humanitarian rationale is the most prominent theme, and interdependence appears as a subtheme throughout the booklet. Comprehensive security is highlighted, receiving a separate chapter. But one is not clear if comprehensive security is the overriding framework for an aid policy that includes humanitarian and interdependence rationales and components, or if comprehensive security is just one of three components of an overall "philosophy of economic cooperation."

A subsequent transformation of the aid philosophy after the booklet's publication confuses the issue even further. Interdependence, the subtheme in the publication, was elevated to a status equal that of humanitarian considerations. Meanwhile, the four reasons for aid cited and explained under the comprehensive security rationale were "transferred" to the interdependence rubric. Today, government officials justify aid to domestic audiences by citing humanitarian considerations and interdependence as the chief reasons why Japan gives aid.[37] Comprehensive national security is sometimes acknowledged but downplayed, except for foreign audiences. What is clear is that comprehensive security and interdependence are separate and distinct conceptually.

A year and a half after the formulation of the aid philosophy, MFA officials were still discussing among themselves the exact relationship between comprehensive security and economic assistance. This problem should be studied, according to one participant in an intraministerial meeting, and he suggested two conceptual possibilities: Place comprehensive security under the interdependence rubric, or place it beside interdependence and humanitarian considerations as a third, additional aid principle.[38] Comprehensive security has been treated in recent years like an orphan at a PTA meeting. Conceptually, Japanese aid policy still reflects to some extent the separation of economics from politics; they are not integrated yet.

The Roots of Ambiguity

The ambiguous and disjointed nature of this aid philosophy reflects the diverse origins of the philosophy's components and the MFA's public relations objectives in formulating these principles. The Japanese economic cooperation philosophy is an eclectic amalgam of ideas already familiar to aid experts. The emphasis on humanitarian considerations owes much to the Pearson Report, which stressed the humanitarian rationale at a time the United States emphasized security purposes, especially in Southeast Asia. The Pearson Report suggested an increase in multilateral aid, then only 10 percent of DAC members' ODA flow. The Jimmy Carter administration, which ended around the same time as the drafting of the Japanese aid philosophy in 1980, stressed a basic human needs approach to aid and channeled 40 percent of ODA to multilateral institutions.

The stress on interdependence reflected the findings of the Brandt Commission, which linked welfare of the South to economic recovery in the North. It noted the zero-growth phenomenon in the developed world in contrast with the 5 to 6 percent growth rates in the developing nations. It argued that if only from a national interest point of view, developed nations should assist the less developed nations. When the Reagan administration took office in 1981, the MFA expected Washington to lean toward the Brandt-interdependence rationale.[39]

While the Pearson and Brandt reports provided working models for aid philosophy drafters, the Foreign Ministry's real concern was the reaction of the Japanese people to the call for greater aid efforts. The MFA's formulation of a philosophy aimed primarily at gaining public understanding and support for economic cooperation, and humanitarian and interdependence rationales were most effective in striking responsive chords among the populace. Quite simply, the booklet constituted an exercise in public relations designed to educate the Japanese people on the need for large aid expenditures in the midst of an economic slowdown. Officials perceived the national consensus on aid as fragile, based largely on ignorance of aid's importance to the nation and on an emotional appeal of helping nations and peoples in need. A 1982 poll conducted by the Prime Minister's Office seems to bear out these feelings. Only 42 percent of those polled expressed familiarity with economic cooperation (of which those who claimed extensive knowledge constituted only 5 percent), with 51 percent admitting a lack of knowledge (39 percent claimed almost total ignorance and 12 percent total ignorance). Seventy percent felt aid is useful and beneficial for recipient nations, but only 59 percent felt that Japan received any benefits.[40]

The polls found comprehensive security to be a popular, or necessary, approach to national security, registering a support rate of 87 percent. When asked about the desirability of specific nonmilitary means of preserving security, stabilization of energy sources (83%), securing foodstuff sources (76%), and promoting peace diplomacy (79%) received high marks. Economic cooperation registered comparatively moderate support (59%) even with the emphasis on its nonmilitary nature under comprehensive security.[41]

Those polled exhibit a strong perception of aid as a purely economic diplomatic tool, question the utility of aid for promoting the national interest, and rank aid below other objectives in promoting security. A Foreign Ministry concerned with maintaining and increasing aid's appeal cannot be expected to take the lead in attempting an explicit integration of aid and security. It will continue to stress humanitarian and interdependence rationales to its own people, and will refer to the strategic rationale gradually, in step with its acceptance by the people of Japan. By the same token the MFA can be expected to emphasize the strategic rationale to foreigners, who have few qualms about Japanese participation in regional and international security efforts through nonmilitary methods.

The Comprehensive National Security Council

The task of integrating conceptually the various components of comprehensive national security was to have fallen not on the Foreign Ministry but on a newly created official organ. The Ohira Study Group *Report* had proposed a Comprehensive National Security Council to serve as the forum for deliberating Japanese security policy. The new Council's mandate consisted of replacing the National Defense Council "as a body for promoting comprehensive and integrated security policy."[42]

Suzuki Zenko assumed office on July 17, 1980. Five days later, he expressed interest in the ministerial council proposal and convened a meeting on July 27 to discuss the Ohira *Report*.[43] He inaugurated the new Ministerial Council on Comprehensive Security on December 2. According to Suzuki, "I established a Comprehensive National Security-related council within the cabinet in December of last year. I am determined through this council, to promote a comprehensive national security policy for our country by promoting the integration of policies in each area."[44]

The cabinet set up an office in the Prime Minister's Office, appointing a councillor and a small staff of personnel on loan from various ministries to oversee the Ministerial Council's administration. The Council is chaired by the chief cabinet secretary and comprises the ministers of finance, Foreign affairs, international trade and industry, transportation, and agriculture, forestry, and fisheries, and the Director generals of the economic planning, defense, and science and technology agencies. Other ministers are to be invited as the occasion demands, and the top executives of the Liberal Democratic Party (the secretary general, the executive secretary, and the chairperson of the Policy Affairs Research Council) are encouraged to attend.[45]

"This new body," wrote one observer soon after its creation, "should it prove successful, may provide the impetus for a more co-ordinated, comprehensive, and rational approach to Japan's own particular security needs."[46] It provided little impetus, however, and proved unsuccessful in promoting the coordination and integration of comprehensive security components either as concept or as policy. The nature, format, and focus of the Ministerial Council hindered the completion of its original mandate.

The Ohira *Report* suggested the replacement of the National Defense Council by the new Ministerial Council.[47] Since this would have entailed Diet approval, the cabinet decided to avoid potential confrontations with suspicious opposition parties and a jurisdiction-conscious bureaucracy. Ministerial councils do not require Diet approval and can be altered or disbanded at the government's will.[48] But questions arose from the beginning concerning the Ministerial Council's status, jurisdiction, and policy-making authority, especially when the National Defense Council existed side by side with the new body to fulfill the same purposes. As one source observed, the new Council "is neither a decisionmaking body nor a consultative organ. The National Defense Council remains the organ in which to deliberate on important matters pertaining to national defense—or respond to emergencies."[49]

Neither was the Ministerial Council's meeting format conducive to action. Gatherings were designed to offer members the opportunity to discuss in an informal and relaxed manner any business at hand. Participants were then free to follow up on any suggestions or ideas gained at the meetings, or, as in most cases, not to pursue ideas. Without a conscious effort to coordinate and integrate the components of comprehensive security, the meetings symbolized the independence of each component of the concept. The government body was not designed to serve as a policy-making unit but as an open discussion forum. From the beginning it did not function as the command post for the conceptualization, coordination, integration, or implementation of comprehensive national security. The Ministerial Council's importance is "symbolic," according to a member of the Prime Minister's Office. It represents the realization of the Japanese people that security is just as important as economic growth and therefore needs careful deliberation by all concerned.[50]

Neither were the foci of discussion at these sessions conducive to the development of an integrated comprehensive security concept. As a general rule, the minister of foreign affairs reported on the international situation as it related to Japanese security. And a look at the meeting agendas reveals a "current events" air of the discussions. Topics seem dictated by upcoming international conferences or a briefing by someone who had just returned from an international gathering. Among topics discussed during the Suzuki years were Poland, the Middle East, the prime minister's visit to Washington, the Soviet party congress, the UN General Assembly meeting, economic problems with the West, U.S.-Japan security consultations, and the national budget.[51]

The problem with these discussion topics was that more suitable forums existed for the same discussions. By not focusing specifically on the coordination and integration of comprehensive security, the Council, in effect, challenged its own raison d'être, especially when it failed to exercise any decision-making authority. The Council ran out of steam under Suzuki. It met four times during the first five months of its creation and only three times during the following year. It lay dormant during the last half year of Suzuki's tenure and the first half year of the Nakasone cabinet.[52]

Prime Minister Nakasone revived the Ministerial Council on Comprehensive Security in 1983 amid widespread suspicion that he had reverted to comprehensive security as a means of softening his strong hawkish image.[53] Nakasone's use of the Council followed the Suzuki pattern. The meeting reviewed the current international situation, including the Williamsburg summit, the Middle East, the OECD's directors' meeting, and the upcoming trip to ASEAN by Nakasone. But the Council still did not function as a forum that looked at the long-term implications of comprehensive security for Japanese foreign policy.

Nakasone took another step in reviving the concept of comprehensive security. He borrowed a page from Ohira's playbook by inaugurating yet another comprehensive security study group in July of 1983. The Peace Problems Research Council (Heiwa Mondai Kenkyukai), like the Ohira study group, was mandated to deliberate security policy. The eleven-member group was composed of experts on diplomacy, economics, finance, energy, and food policy. Sensitive defense topics were to be major topics of discussion, including the 1 percent of GNP defense spending limit. To soften the impression that Nakasone's real intent was to use his study group as a smokescreen to build up the military, Chief Cabinet Secretary Gotoda Masaharu pointed out that "There are no experts on defense and military problems among the members of the Peace Problems Research Council. They are amateurs."[49] Gotoda maintained that the group is expected to approach the question of defense from the viewpoint of the ordinary citizen; its purpose was "to exchange views from a broader point of view for the promotion of a comprehensive security policy."[54]

In many ways a review of the premises of the Ohira Study Group was overdue even though only a few years had passed since the publication of the *Report*. The environment that gave birth to Ohira's group had experienced a transformation. The Iranian hostage crises ended; Japan adjusted well to the second oil crisis of 1979 but faced fiscal difficulties not foreseen by the study group; the Asian region settled into a state of tense stability after Afghanistan and Kampuchea; the new Reagan administration entered office in 1981 committed to rebuilding U.S. military power and restoring economic strength at home and abroad; Reagan also reaffirmed U.S. commitments to allies; and in Japan, the defense debate widened amid a growing convergence among political forces toward a rough consensus on the preservation of the peace Constitution, the legitimacy of the Self-Defense Force and the acceptability of the U.S.-Japan Security Treaty.

The final recommendations of the Peace Problems Research Council reveal moderation rather than a radical break with past security policy measures. Opposition parties accused the study group of supporting Nakasone's hawkish inclinations, including a revamping of defense policy and the abandonment of the 1 percent of GNP defense spending limit. Qualitative and limited quantitative improvements in defense policy, however, have been subjects of discussion in Japan since the 1970s and appeared in Ohira's comprehensive security report of 1980. Nakasone's study group advocates changes in defense policy but within the standard framework of maintaining the peace Constitution, the exclusively defensive defense policy, the three nonnuclear principles, U.S.-Japan security cooperation, and civilian control over the military. The Nakasone group warns against provoking fear of a remilitarized Japan among neighboring Asian countries and encourages the government to gain the understanding and support of the Japanese people for its security policy.[55]

The Nakasone Research Council explicitly endorses the multidimensional comprehensive security approach, including a positive aid policy. It insists that Japan expand its political role in world affairs and use its economic capabilities to support and help manage the international economic system. The report asserts that Japan's contribution to international society as an "international nation-state" *(kokusai kokka)* is in the national interest. Methods of preserving the national interest include serving as a major supplier of international capital, opening domestic markets to foreign goods and capital, and stockpiling oil and other critical natural resources.

As for economic assistance policy, the Research Council urges the government to improve its aid record. At a minimum the government must fulfill its pledge to double aid in five years and must increase aid expenditures as a percentage of GNP to at least the DAC average.[56] These recommendations were predictable and relatively uncontroversial.

Press reports make no mention of any detailed treatment of the economic aid-security policy relationship. To the contrary the method by which the Research Council chose to release its findings makes it clear that military and nonmilitary security questions were discussed separately. The Council released its findings and recommendations on nonmilitary aspects as an interim report in March 1984. It then issued its recommendations for military defense policy as part of the final report in December. Nakasone's group followed the usual practice of separating rather than attempting to integrate military and nonmilitary implications and methods. For economic aid policy, the result seems to be the continued consideration of aid primarily as a North-South issue and the usual preoccupation with amounts rather than rationale.

At this point in postwar Japanese history, the integration of economic assistance and security policies seems impossible *conceptually* because of domestic political problems for the government. But the irony is that strategic aid *policy* is alive and well despite conceptual ambiguity, or maybe because of it. The use of aid for political and strategic reasons became an entrenched feature of the Ohira, Suzuki, and Nakasone cabinets.

Notes

1. Gerald L. Curtis, "Japanese Security Policies and the United States," *Foreign Affairs* (Spring 1981):853.

2. Ibid., pp. 863–4.

3. James William Morley, "A Time for Realism in the Military Defense of Japan," in Franklin Weinstein, ed., *U.S.-Japan Relations and the Security of East Asia: The Next Decade* (Boulder, Colo.: Westview Press, 1978), p. 54.

4. Makoto Momoi, "Are There Any Alternative Strategies for the Defense of Japan?" ibid., p. 78.

5. Curtis, "Japanese Security," p. 853.

6. Ken Matsui, *Keizai Kyoryoku; Towareru Nihon no Keizai Gaiko* (Tokyo: Yuhikaku, 1983), p. 5.

7. Toshio Shishido, *Tonan Ajia Enjo o Kangaeru* (Tokyo: Toyo Keizai Shimposha, 1973), p. 29.

8. Klaus Knorr, *The Power of Nations: The Political Economy of International Relations* (New York: Basic Books, 1975), pp. 169–70.

9. Ibid., p. 170.

10. Quoted in Koichiro Matsuura, "Japan's Cooperative Relations with ASEAN," *Mainichi Daily News,* September 30, 1981.

11. *Asahi Shimbun,* January 12, 1983.

12. *Asahi Shimbun,* February 22, 1983.

13. Anzen Hosho Kenkyukai, *Ekonomisuto ga Kaita Sogo Anzen Hosho no Kozu* (Tokyo: Nihon Seisansei Honbu, 1981), pp. 10, 213–15.

14. Matsuura, "Cooperative Relations."

15. Saburo Okita, "Japan Should Rethink Its Aid to Southeast Asia," *Asian Wall Street Journal*, June 24–25, 1983.

16. Interview, May 23, 1983.

17. Quoted in J.W.M. Chapman, R. Drifte, and I.T.M. Gow, *Japan's Quest for Comprehensive Security: Defense, Diplomacy and Dependence* (New York: St. Martin's Press, 1982), p. xvi.

18. In Robert W. Barnett, *Beyond War: Japan's Concept of Comprehensive National Security* (Washington and New York: Pergamon Brassey's International Defense Publishers, 1984), p. 85.

19. Morley, "Realism," p. 52.

20. Nobutoshi Akao, ed., *Japan's Economic Security* (New York: St. Martin's Press, 1983), pp. 6–7.

21. Kiichi Saeki, "Nihon no Anzen Hosho," in Hiromi Arisawa, ed., *Nihon Keizai to Sogo Anzen Hosho* (Tokyo: Tokyo Daigaku Shuppankai, 1981), pp. 42–3.

22. Comprehensive National Security Study Group, *Report on Comprehensive National Security* (Tokyo: Prime Minister's Office, 1980).

23. Mike Mochizuki, "Japan's Search for Strategy," *International Security*, Winter 1983–84, pp. 159–60. He distinguishes "political realists" from "unarmed neutralists," "Japanese Gaullists," and "military realists." Mochizuki does note that the ideas of political realists and military realists are sometimes indistinguishable.

24. Ibid.

25. Comprehensive National Security Study Group, *Report*, p. 33.

26. Ibid., p. 32.

27. Ibid., p. 33.

28. Ibid.

29. Ibid., p. 21.

30. Ibid., p. 10.

31. Japan, Ministry of Foreign Affairs, "Anzen Hosho no Gunji-men to Hi-Gunji-men (Toku ni, Anzen Hosho Kara Mita Keizai Kyoryoku no Ichizuke," April 1982.

32. Chapman, Drifte, and Gow, *Japan's Quest*, p. xvi.

33. Alan Rix, *Japan's Economic Aid* (New York: St. Martin's Press, 1980).

34. Japan, Ministry of Foreign Affairs, Keizai Kyoryoku Kyoku, and Keizai Kyoryoku Kenkyukai, *Keizai Kyoryoku no Rinen—Seifu Kaihatsu Enjo wa Naze Okonau no ka* (Tokyo: Zaidan Hojin Kokusai Kyoryoku Suishin Kyokai, 1981).

35. Ibid., pp. 76–83.

36. Ibid., pp. 83–4.

37. For example, see Koichiro Matsuura, "Japan's Role in International Cooperation," *National Development* (September 1981).

38. Japan, Ministry of Foreign Affairs, "Gunji-men," p. 4.

39. Koichiro Matsuura, "Sogo Anzen Hosho Seisaku toshite no Keizai Kyoryoku," speech delivered before the Sogo Anzen Chosakai, Dai Yon-kai Kenkyukai, April 4, 1981, pp. 3–5.

40. Japan, Prime Minister's Office, *Waga Kuni no Heiwa Anzen ni Kansuru Yoron Chosa*, August 1982, pp. 14–16.

41. Ibid., pp. 7–8.

42. Comprehensive National Security Study Group, *Report,* p. 72.

43. See Yuichiro Nagatomi, *Kindai o Koete: Ko-Ohira Sori no Nokosareta Mono,* vol. 2 (Tokyo: Okura Zaimu Kyokai, 1983), pp. 50–4.

44. Ibid., p. 53.

45. Japan, Ministry of Foreign Affairs, Chosa Kikakubu, *Anzen Hosho Mondai Handobukku,* March 1982, pp. 44–5.

46. I.T.M. Gow, "Part One: Defence," in Chapman, Drifte, and Gow, *Japan's Quest,* p. 1.

47. Comprehensive National Security Study Group, *Report,* p. 72.

48. Gow, "Defence," pp. 75–7.

49. Research Institute for Peace and Security, *Asian Security 1982* (Tokyo: Nikkei Business Publishing Company, 1982), p. 151.

50. Interview, June 10, 1983.

51. Japan, Ministry of Foreign Affairs, *Handobukku,* pp. 44–6.

52. It met in December (twice) of 1980; March, April, and October of 1981; and January and May of 1982. See ibid., pp. 45–6.

53. *Nihon Keizai Shimbun,* May 25, 1983; *Yomiuri Shimbun,* May 24 and 25, 1983; and *Asahi Shimbun,* May 2, 1983.

54. On the Research Council, see *Asahi Shimbun,* July 28 and August 6, 1983; *Nihon Keizai Shimbun,* July 28, 1983; and *Tokyo Shimbun,* July 23, 1983.

55. For a summary of the Council's findings, see *Asahi Shimbun,* December 19, 1984 and *Nihon Keizai Shimbun,* December 19, 1984.

56. See *Asahi Shimbun,* March 15, 1984, for a summary of the Council's recommendations for economic and other nonmilitary sectors.

3
Strategic Aid as Policy

> Japan should be a Santa Claus to everybody.
> —An ASEAN Ambassador to Japan
>
> Japan has been increasing its aid to those areas which are important
> for the maintenance of world peace and stability. Which particular
> countries are to be included in such areas is independently judged by
> Japan, taking into account the prevailing international situation.
> —from *Japan's Official Development
> Assistance 1984 Annual Report*

The Ohira Masayoshi cabinet initiated the formulation of a comprehensive national security concept that propounded the desirability of politicizing economic aid policy. Even before Ohira's Study Group submitted its report, however, the prime minister had already embarked on an active policy of extending aid to specific recipients for political and security-related purposes. In other words, the debut of strategic aid policy *preceded* the conceptualization of comprehensive security and its adoption as national policy. Neither comprehensive security nor the Foreign Ministry's new aid philosophy gave birth to or justified the existence of strategic aid. It entered the world as a policy in search of a rationale. In fact, the government formulated two additional "philosophies" or rationales separate and distinct from comprehensive security, humanitarian considerations and interdependence, to explain and justify strategic aid.

Strategic aid commenced as ad hoc, case-by-case policy measures that responded to immediate foreign policy needs. It emerged as a policy with a rationale, target countries, and pace defined in part by others. The policy, therefore, fails to present a coherent vision of long-term directions and objectives. It is a policy that ran ahead of the domestic consensus on economic cooperation. The government has exhibited caution and even some reluctance as a result in the handling of strategic aid. As a consequence the policy has developed with fluctuations, seeming inconsistencies, and qualifications in implementation.

The domestic political, legal, and emotional restrictions on the unfettered use of political aid explains in large part the ups and downs of policy implementation. But those who encourage Japan to continue and expand the policy should also take into consideration the genuine doubts in the minds of Japanese leaders concerning the implications of strategic aid for future Japanese foreign policy. For many Japanese leaders mirror the people's reluctance to abandon the economic and humanitarian rationales of aid policy, shrink from the prospect of a globally oriented policy that may sacrifice the concentration on the Asian region, and worry about the massive amount of capital needed to finance an expanding aid policy. Strategic aid has come far in a short while given its restricted domestic environment but not smoothly or with a clear rationale for its existence.

Countries Bordering Conflict

Japanese strategic assistance debuted in 1978 and 1979 amid the Soviet invasion of Afghanistan, the Vietnamese incursion into Kampuchea, the Iranian hostage crisis, the Camp David accords between Egypt and Israel, and the Sino-Japanese Treaty of Peace and Friendship. The Ohira cabinet significantly increased ODA to specific nations deemed strategically and politically important to Japanese and Western interests. Ohira doubled aid to Thailand and increased flows to Pakistan by 3.7 times and to Turkey by almost 10 times the previous year's total. Between 1977 and 1980 Tokyo supplied $442 million to Egypt, the fifth largest recipient of Japanese aid at the time, and Ohira inaugurated foreign aid to China by pledging $1.5 billion during his visit to Beijing.[1]

Ohira stated in his January 1980 policy address that "For the purpose of maintaining the stability of neighboring countries in the area, particularly Pakistan, we would like to give positive consideration, in cooperation with U.S. and Western European countries, to the request from these countries for cooperation in the economic field."[2] Foreign Minister Sonoda Sunao left for Pakistan in March as Ohira's special envoy and pledged to more than double the amount of aid Japan supplied in 1979. In April, at an OECD-sponsored emergency conference on Turkey, Japan pledged $100 million in yen loans and export credits to Ankara. "The announcement was made," according to Japan's *Diplomatic Bluebook,* "in view of the economic difficulties facing Turkey, the strategic position it holds in the Middle East, and Japanese cooperation with the United States and West European nations."

In April the government announced its intention to grant 57 billion yen to Thailand: "Aid to Thailand was increased, partly because that nation is a member of ASEAN, which receives a major portion of Japanese assistance, and partly because it was troubled by the influx of Indochinese refugees."[3] Japan had pledged $10 million to the UN high commissioner for refugees in 1978, an increase of 10 times the previous year's contribution, to assist Vietnamese refugees, including the "boat people."[4]

The government did not justify this abrupt departure from the "separation of politics from economics" aid approach by relying on the comprehensive security rationale. Interdependence, humanitarian considerations, and comprehensive security had yet to be formulated as interrelated components of an official aid philosophy. Instead, the government created the concept of aid to "countries bordering areas of conflict" (*funso shuhen koku*) to cover Thailand, Pakistan, and Turkey. Under the "countries bordering areas of conflict" formula, Thailand received $688 million between 1978 and 1981, elevating Bangkok to the position of the second largest recipient of Japanese aid after Indonesia during this period. Pakistan received $445 million, seventh on the top 10 list, while Turkey broke into the top 10 for the first time in 1981 (with $51.4 million that year).[5]

While increasing aid to the three countries bordering areas of conflict, the Ohira cabinet denied aid to a country perceived as causing conflict. In 1979 the government froze a $70 million aid program to Vietnam in protest against the invasion and occupation of Kampuchea. Japan had departed from past practices by using aid overtly as a diplomatic weapon.

The extension of aid to countries bordering conflict and the freeze to Hanoi constituted decisive steps for an economic giant previously hesitant to flex its political muscles. But this decisiveness can be questioned upon closer examination of Japanese behavior at that time. For these steps begin to appear as a reaction to the heat of the moment, a heat that Suzuki Zenko apparently did his utmost to cool.

One might argue that the extension of aid to countries bordering areas of conflict and the economic sanction against Vietnam do not indicate a radical break with past aid policy or an unqualified resoluteness in Ohira's diplomatic stance. With respect to Thailand and Pakistan, Japan has traditionally concentrated its aid distribution in the Asian region; therefore, aid to these two Asian nations hardly represents a change in aid policy direction. Furthermore, Islamabad and Bangkok have consistently ranked among the top 10 recipients of Tokyo's assistance since the 1960s. Pakistan and Thailand ranked third and seventh in 1968, fourth and seventh in 1974, and tenth and fifth in 1978.[6] From this perspective the only real difference seems to be the amount of aid.

The Ohira cabinet's decisiveness toward Pakistan and Thailand also seems overshadowed by the apparently reactive nature of the move to increase aid. The United States designated both nations as frontline states against Soviet actions in Afghanistan and a perceived Soviet-inspired Vietnamese invasion of Kampuchea, and Washington urged allies to pursue punitive policies toward Moscow. One Reagan administration official stated that

> Pakistan is now a front-line state facing 85,000 Soviet soldiers across its borders in Afghanistan. Pakistan's strategic location at the eastern flank of

the Persian Gulf, makes it very important that we and our allies undertake a
major effort to help Pakistan resist Soviet pressures to become stronger and
more self-confident.[7]

The Carter administration offered Islamabad $400 million in military and
economic aid for 1981 and 1982, which was rejected by the Pakistani president as "peanuts."[8] The new Reagan administration announced a $3 billion
aid package in June 1981.[9]

Tokyo showed more enthusiasm toward Thailand, which received close
to 70 percent of its total aid from Japan in 1981 ($214.5 million).[10] But then,
Thailand is a member of ASEAN, which received one-third of Japan's total
ODA during the Ohira years. Foreign Ministry officials assert that Tokyo
has developed a special relationship with Bangkok based on political interests. Only Indonesia topped Thailand in terms of the total amount of aid
Japan disbursed between 1978 and 1981 ($618.63 million for Thailand),[11] but
in 1982 aid commitments to Thailand exceeded commitments to Indonesia
and in 1983 net disbursement figures reveal that, for the first time, Thailand
received more aid than Indonesia ($248.12 million versus $235.46 million).[12]
However, many officials interviewed deny Thailand's frontline status, citing
humanitarian considerations (refugees and the plight of farmers in the
northeast) and interdependence (especially the "multilateral" nature of aid
to all ASEAN members).[13]

Some Japanese officials deny that Japan merely followed U.S. dictates.
They argue that these Japanese actions represent a diplomatic initiative
taken in the absence of a decisive U.S. policy at the time. One official points
out that Ohira acted during a time when President Carter experienced
political difficulties with the Pakistani government (over nuclear fuel pro-
cessing and human rights issues).[14] A U.S. government official looked back
to those days and noted:

> We do make specific suggestions. But on some, we didn't need arm-twisting.
> On some they were cautious. On Thailand, they did see commercial inter-
> ests and general security; that is, they did see a regional security interest. . . .
> We urged them to give to Pakistan, but they didn't need any urging. It was
> clear that Afghanistan posed a threat—oil supplies, Soviet warm water
> ports to the south, etc.[15]

The case of Turkey is more clear-cut. Japan's decision to increase financial support came in large part as a response to urgings from the United
States, which extended Ankara $450 million in 1980 and $547 million in
1981,[16] and especially from West Germany. Bonn placed special political
emphasis on Turkey and extended 10 percent of its bilateral ODA to Ankara.
At a June 1981 bilateral aid meeting, Japan reaffirmed its support for
Turkey, but Japanese officials assured domestic audiences about the limits

of Japan's commitment. A Foreign Ministry official explained at a session of the Ministerial Council on Comprehensive Security that Japan cannot assist a NATO country in the same way as Asian nations.[17]

Turkey proved more difficult to justify because of the thin commercial and direct security links with Japan. It stood as a country bordering conflict without a conflict raging on its immediate border, and thus this gives the impression of being grafted onto the "conflict" formula after strong West German pressure. The government now stresses the interdependence and some humanitarian rationales within a multilateral framework. That is, Japan downplays the bilateral nature of Turkish aid by maintaining that it was a response to and cooperation with OECD (and definitely not NATO) efforts to bolster Turkey's troubled economy.

The Japanese, in other words, began to soften their toughened image immediately after formulating and implementing the aid to "countries bordering areas of conflict" formula. Even the cut-off of aid to Vietnam proved conditional and partial. While the government froze the aid package, it allowed a trickle to continue on humanitarian grounds, in the form of technical assistance to a hospital outside Ho Chi Minh City, which the Japanese built under the previous South Vietnamese government. Japan attempted to keep the door open to a dialogue with Hanoi and expressed a willingness to resume aid and to contribute to economic reconstruction upon Vietnamese withdrawal from Kampuchea. Tokyo also supported the succession of the Vietnamese government to the seat previously occupied by the South Vietnamese regime in the Asian Development Bank (ADB) and subsequently supported, unsuccessfully against American objections, efforts to resume ADB loans to Vietnam.

The greatest testimony to Tokyo's hesitation in openly linking aid and security is the fact that the policy concept of aid to "countries bordering areas of conflict" has never been used again to justify economic assistance. It remains a historical oddity of the Ohira years, limited in usage to the three countries, Turkey, Pakistan, and Thailand. Aid to such countries as Egypt, Oman, North Yemen, Sudan, and Jamaica expanded thereafter under similar political and strategic criteria. But the Suzuki cabinet made certain that the packaging of security-related assistance exhibited a lighter strategic coloring.

The Suzuki Method

The impression that Suzuki sought to use comprehensive security to deemphasize the importance of military defense efforts by substituting nonmilitary security methods is difficult to avoid. In his January 1981 policy address to the Diet, he stated that "Given the current international situation and Japan's position, it is obvious that it is difficult to insure Japan's peace and safety merely by increased defense capabilities."[18] While acknowledging the importance of the U.S. security arrangement, the prime minister also stressed that "Japan, in its role as an active contributor to peace and development in the world, intends to redouble its efforts to cooperate with the developing nations."[19]

Suzuki personally raised economic assistance to the status of pillar of Japanese foreign policy under the comprehensive national security policy concept. One of his first acts was the creation of the Ministerial Council on Comprehensive Security, and at the Council's second meeting in December 1980, he took an initiative on aid policy that resulted in the cabinet's adoption of the second aid-doubling plan that would replace the successful doubling effort of 1977–1980. Suzuki announced this New Medium Term Target in January 1981. The Target expected an increase in Japan's aggregate aid disbursement total to $21.4 billion over five years, to the level of 0.7 percent of GNP.[20]

Suzuki's dovish tendencies were on display during his May 1981 visit to Washington. The prime minister pledged greater efforts to improve Japanese sea and air defense capabilities in the Reagan-Suzuki joint communiqué, but as one analyst observes, "This language was particularly well suited to Prime Minister Suzuki's needs. In answering questions in Japan he could simultaneously favor defense burden sharing and yet point out that Japan was not bound to any specific military missions or expenditures."[21] But the communiqué referred to the U.S.-Japan relationship as an "alliance," a term usually avoided in joint statements. At a news conference Suzuki reacted impulsively and instinctively by denying that "alliance" carried a military connotation: "The idea of a military alliance is not contained in the joint communiqué." Suzuki maintained that alliance referred to cultural relations and went further by denying that Japan had made commitments to the United States on the defense of sea-lanes. Division of roles, according to the prime minister, did not refer to military roles.[22]

"It was an embarrassing news conference," states one American analyst. "There were a number of crucial moments during which Prime Minister Suzuki appeared to be repudiating the communiqué that he had just issued with President Reagan, as well as the basic thrust of the discussions on defense issues that had taken place between Japanese and American officials from January to May."[23] Japanese sources also shared a similar impression: Since the Suzuki cabinet did not seem to expend great energy toward actually increasing defense efforts after returning home, opting for "minimalism, gradual concessions made under foreign pressure," it "even gave the impression that it was turning back, even if temporarily, from the pledges given in May 1981."[24]

While most attention focused on the "alliance" flap, the joint communiqué is also noteworthy because it established the outline and guidelines for

Japan's aid policy, including strategic aid policy. First, it affirmed Japan's intention to play an active role in Asia. Suzuki pledged

> to continue respectively to expand cooperative relations with the People's Republic of China;
>
> to promote the maintenance of peace on the Korean peninsula as important for peace and security in East Asia, including Japan;
>
> to continue their cooperation in support of the solidarity of ASEAN and its quest for the greater resilience and developments of its members.[25]

The People's Republic of China, the Republic of Korea, and the ASEAN states form the core of Japan's economic assistance policy today.

Second, Suzuki's pledge reflected and portended the increasingly globalized focus of Japanese foreign policy and the basis for strategic aid policy:

> The President and Prime Minister affirmed that the maintenance of peace and security in the Middle East, particularly in the Gulf region, is highly important for the peace and security of the entire world. ... The President and the Prime Minister took note of the presence of various elements of instability in other areas of the world, and particularly with respect to some parts of Africa and Central America, they expressed their concern about the existence of conditions affecting peace and stability.[26]

Finally, paragraph 9 embodied the Suzuki version of strategic aid and aid to "countries bordering areas of conflict":

> They affirmed that political, economic and social stability of developing countries is indispensable for the maintenance of peace and stability of the world. The Prime Minister stated that the Government of Japan will strive to expand and improve its official development assistance under the New Medium Term Target and that the Government will strengthen its aid to those areas which are important to the maintenance of peace and stability of the world.[27]

From this point on, under Suzuki, the terms used in the last sentence of this paragraph, "areas which are important to the maintenance of peace and stability of the world," became the catchphrase for strategic aid. It superceded the "countries bordering conflict" formulation, limited to only three nations. The new slogan has increased both flexibility and ambiguity. The focus shifted from "countries" to a less defined "areas." It has softened strategic aid's image and changed the nuance of its objective. Aid no longer connotes involvement in "conflict" but in a more pacific and vague maintenance of world "peace." What is the difference between "countries bordering conflict" and "areas which are important to the maintenance of peace and stability of the world?" In interviews government officials admit that in practice they are one, cut from the same cloth.

For the Suzuki cabinet, the distinction was significant. If the cabinet appeared to retreat from the military aspects of comprehensive security and commitments to the Reagan administration, it sought to compensate by exhibiting a willingness of contribute to regional and international security through the extension of economic aid. But Suzuki preferred to carry out this commitment without attaching an overt strategic tinge to aid policy. Observers assumed, therefore, that political aid had suffered a severe setback. As one Japanese aid expert writes, "the 'politicization of aid' that had been steadily pushed until the end of 1980 was temporarily halted."[28] Rather, according to another observer, Suzuki "stressed the importance of socioeconomic development of Asian countries and argued at Cancun that ODA should play the central role in economic cooperation extended to developing countries."[29] The denuding of strategic considerations, according to some analysts, sidelined Suzuki's effort to gain acceptance abroad for comprehensive security:

> The concept has failed ... to win sympathy from the international community, which tends to regard it as an arrangement designed to keep defense spending low, so that a perception gap concerning security developed in 1981.
> The gap arises partly because Japan refuses to take military implications into account in its economic cooperation, though economic cooperation is part of what it calls "comprehensive security."[30]

The most outstanding and widely reported example of Suzuki's hesitation on acknowledging strategic uses of economic aid was the case of South Korea. In the summer of 1981 the Chun Doo Hwan government demanded a Japanese aid package of $10 billion. The demand stunned Tokyo not only because of the staggering amount but also because of the rationale. Seoul reasoned that since Korea devotes 6 percent of its GNP and over one-third of its national budget to defense efforts that directly benefit Japan as well, Tokyo should help defray the cost. The Koreans reduced the figure to $6 billion in August and dropped the security rationale in November, but the initial demand had established an indelible image in the minds of the Japanese people: Korea wants security aid. The often acrimonious negotiations remained deadlocked throughout Suzuki's tenure. The official breakthrough occurred in January 1983, with a $4 billion settlement and a historic visit to Seoul by Suzuki's successor, Nakasone Yasuhiro.[31]

Suzuki had pledged "to promote the maintenance of peace on the Korean peninsula" in Washington in 1981 and at the Ottawa summit that summer. The Chun government called Suzuki's hand and Suzuki folded, according to many interpretations. But for the Japanese numerous problems plagued the Korean request beside the amount and security rationale. These included the composition of Seoul's aid demand (eventually $3.5 billion in yen loans and $2.5 billion in commodity credits); the lack of specific Korean projects (Japanese aid is project-oriented); the feeling that Korea, a newly industrializing country (NIC), should not receive massive amounts of ODA (but should continue to rely on private sector sources); personality clashes between negotiators (especially with Foreign Minister Lho Shin Yong); questions about providing aid to an unstable Chun government (which became involved in a billion dollar scandal involving Chun's wife); the severing under Chun of informal, private channels that had fostered close ties between business and government elites during the Park Chung Hee era; the problems of budgeting ODA beyond one-year intervals (the Koreans specified a five-year time frame); the persistence of the Kim Dae Jung issue (the Chun government sentenced opposition leader Kim to death but later commuted it to life imprisonment, both actions a violation, in Tokyo's view, of a political agreement reached after Kim's 1974 abduction from a Tokyo hotel); and the eruption of the "textbook crisis" in the summer of 1982 (over proposed changes by the Japanese Education Ministry to soften depictions in high school history texts of Japanese behavior in China, Southeast Asia, and Korea during World War II).[32]

The standard interpretation of the aid imbroglio puts the onus on Suzuki, depicted as balking on strategic aid, and credits Nakasone with forging the breakthrough based on a positive attitude toward strategic aid for Korea. One scholar writes,

> The Suzuki government's inability to resolve the loan issue should be attributed largely to its rigid interpretation of Japan's foreign aid objectives, whereas the Nakasone government's ability to settle the issue reflected the latter's willingness to interpret Japanese foreign aid more liberally as an instrument of its foreign policy. The different approaches of the two prime ministers to the same economic aid issue stemmed from their differing perceptions of the security link between Japan and South Korea.[33]

A Japanese journalist comments,

> Suzuki was coutious [sic] about making commitments to Korea as the latter's "security" rationale behind the $6 billion request seemed politically questionable and economically excessive.
>
> Mr. Nakasone, on the other hand, put Korea high atop his priority list, visiting that country in January shortly after he had become Prime Minister. As a result, he finally settled the economic cooperation issue that had been pending for a year and a half. By agreeing to provide $4 billion to Korea . . . it has become clear that the security element will play a pivotal role in the Nakasone Cabinet's foreign aid policy.[34]

The problem with this interpretation is that it ignores the hesitation and caution on Korean assistance under both Suzuki and Nakasone. Nakasone's *attitude* toward and willingness to use aid for strategic purposes may have differed from a more reluctant Suzuki, but his cabinet's *policy* approach reveals only slight differences. Suzuki favored aid as a substitute, and not a supplement, for military defense efforts. His objection to the Korean aid stemmed from the linkage in the popular consciousness between aid and Korea's military defense policy. He thus sought to soften the strategic coloring of aid policy lest it threaten the domestic consensus on overall economic aid policy. Nakasone's positive attitude toward strategic aid, however, did not mean an unconditional surrender to Korean demands.

The Nakasone Style and the Korean Aid Settlement

Nakasone's hawkish image deepened upon entering office in November 1982 through a series of actions and statements. In December he approved the transfer of military technology to the United States, placing Washington outside the restrictions on military technology transfers abroad. During his January visit to Washington, he declared his intention to convert the Japanese ship of state into an aircraft carrier against Soviet missiles and Backfire bombers. He also linked Japan and the United States in a "common destiny", raising the specter in Japan of marching arm in arm toward a possible nuclear armageddon. Nakasone took a more forthcoming attitude toward sea-lane defense and the acceptance of a wider role sharing with the United States. He expressed a willingness to blockade the three straits surrounding Japan that led to the open seas in times of crisis and to escort American vessels to Japan during emergencies.

These positions raised eyebrows and opposition ire at home. However, Nakasone soon began to soften his image amid local elections during the spring and a House of Councillor's election in June 1983. A long-time advocate of constitutional revision, Nakasone pledged to preserve the peace Constitution as prime minister despite his personal beliefs. After some hesitation he also accepted the three nonnuclear principles (against the manufacture, possession, and allowing the entry into Japanese territory of nuclear weapons). Despite his personal belief in the need for higher defense spending, his cabinet has maintained the policy of spending less than 1 percent of GNP. Annual defense spending increases under the "hawkish" Nakasone cabinet have remained below "dovish" Suzuki cabinet levels: 7.6 and 7.8 percent under Suzuki and 6.5, 6.65, and 6.9 percent under Nakasone. Nakasone repeatedly stressed "dovish" positions during his swing through the ASEAN region in spring 1983: Japan will not become a military power; it will pursue exclusively defensive defense within the framework of the peace

Constitution and the three nonnuclear principles.[35] These are positions indistinguishable from Suzuki's cabinet. After a year in office Japanese journalists began to record a change in tone and attitude in Nakasone's personality, from initial aloofness to a "humble Nakasone" or a "polite prime minister" more willing to listen to the voices of the people and opposition parties.[36]

Like Suzuki, Nakasone also found the comprehensive national security concept useful. He reconvened the Ministerial Council on Comprehensive Security in spring 1983, after a one-year hiatus, and formed the Peace Problems Research Council in July. In December the ruling Liberal Democratic Party (LDP) suffered a stunning setback in the House of Representatives election. Nakasone barely avoided a situation of parity in the Diet between the LDP and opposition parties by forging a coalition with the small conservative New Liberal Club, which advocates the use of economic assistance as a major foreign policy pillar. Nakasone appointed a member of the Ohira–Suzuki faction as director general of the Defense Agency, who immediately revived the memory of Ohira Masayoshi and the appropriateness of the comprehensive security approach for Japan.[37]

Cynics may contend that these moves constitute blatant efforts at public relations, an "image change," as the Japanese might say, rather than deeply held convictions, or efforts to cloak a military buildup with a nonmilitary smokescreen. However, Nakasone had gone on record in favor of comprehensive security before becoming prime minister and before its adoption by Suzuki as national policy. In 1978, Nakasone endorsed comprehensive security principles:

> In as much as the traditional causes of war are disappearing among advanced nations, the major objective of armament has shifted from fighting and winning wars to deterring war. ...
>
> A nation's security is maintained by a combination of diplomatic efforts, economic cooperation, the building of international public opinion, resources policy, and other elements, with national consensus and will as the foundation. The so-called defense of Japan, with the SDF as its core, is only a small part of such a comprehensive security policy and is intended for use only in the event of extreme emergency to deter or repel aggression.[38]

Nakasone even proposed a new "comprehensive security expenditures" item in the national budget, with 3 percent of GNP allocated to "international cultural exchange, economic cooperation, the stockpiling of oil and food, and the development of certain areas of science and technology."[39] Nakasone also provided a ringing endorsement of economic assistance policy under a comprehensive security framework:

> The Japanese government's overseas development aid (ODA) is much too small. Prime Minister Fukuda said recently that the government intends to

double ODA in three years, but the amount, since it is reckoned in dollars, is bound to increase automatically due to yen appreciation. What Japan should actually do is not engage in such mathematical tricks but increase ODA to such an extent as to astound Europe and the United States, expanding its economic, cultural, and scientific contributions to cover every part of the world. Such efforts, I believe, will contribute to the comprehensive security policy for Japan and the world ... and also to efforts to ensure world peace.[40]

Among Nakasone's "brains," close advisers outside the LDP and his faction, are strong supporters of comprehensive national security. These "political realists" include Sato Seizaburo of Tokyo University and Kosaka Masataka of Kyoto University. Both served on Ohira's Study Group on Comprehensive National Security, and Kosaka chaired Nakasone's Peace Problems Research Council. Nakasone brings to the prime minister's office familiarity with and acceptance of comprehensive security; they are not strangers.

In Nakasone's first policy speech in December 1982, he endorsed the New Medium Term Target aid-doubling plan and provided the following statement on Japan's security.

Our basic stance on security is to maintain the Japan-U.S. security arrangements and to seek to achieve a high defense capability limited to that necessary for self defense.

At the same time, we will pay due attention so as to not become a military power and not to pose any threat to neighboring countries. ...

Moreover, I believe it is necessary from the perspective of comprehensive security policy that we promote a variety of integrated measures including those to further develop free trade, to secure stable supplies of resources, energy and foodstuffs, and to enrich economic cooperation in order to ensure peace and security for Japan.[41]

This statement could have been delivered by Ohira or Suzuki. It contains the current, basic tenets of Japanese security policy upheld by all recent Japanese cabinets. Emphases and nuances may differ, but the direction remains steady. Suzuki may have stressed the nonmilitary aspects more than Nakasone, but, by the same token, Nakasone may be returning to Ohira's "balanced chain links" view. From this perspective defense capability is the weak link in the comprehensive security chain and therefore requires strengthening in order to equal economic and other nonmilitary capabilities. Such is the beauty of comprehensive security as a political symbol and slogan. In short Nakasone has not abandoned nonmilitary security considerations in favor of a defense buildup; assertiveness is mixed with caution, tempered by the need to respond to public and opposition concerns. One can now take another look at Nakasone's handling of the South Korean aid issue.

Prime Minister Suzuki would probably not have journeyed across the Sea of Japan to Seoul had he remained in office. Nakasone's decision reflected his personal interest in improving relations with Korea. The economic cooperation issue would have been settled under Suzuki without his successor's shuttle diplomacy, and the agreement may not have differed much from Nakasone's accomplishment.

First, Japanese and Korean negotiators compromised on the $4 billion figure by June 1982, under the Suzuki cabinet, but the textbook crisis that erupted in July and August hindered any final agreement. The issue was settled in December, just prior to Nakasone's visit in January (and was probably a precondition for the visit), but the final settlement hardly satisfied the Koreans despite Nakasone's apparent eagerness to mend fences. By then Korea preferred $2.3 billion in low-interest yen loans and $1.7 billion in commodity credits, but the Japanese side prevailed: $1.8 billion in yen loans, no commodity loans, and $2.15 billion in harder Export Import Bank credits. The Koreans hoped for a four percent interest rate on the Export Import Bank loans but had to settle for six percent. Seoul preferred the disbursement of the $4 billion dollars to be accomplished in five years but had to settle for seven. Finally the Japanese expect 70 percent of the aid to be tied to Japanese procurement. The terms and conditions of the aid agreement were highly favorable to Japan.[42]

One may have expected greater largess on the aid terms from a cabinet that seemingly sought a closer security-related relationship with Korea. But the Nakasone cabinet remained circumspect on security issues and on the security implications of the economic assistance. The Japanese refusal of commodity aid was based on fears that the Koreans would convert commodity credits to defense-related uses. These loans are usually extended to the neediest of countries with balance-of-payments problems to enable them to purchase and import specific commodities. They have little impact on long-term development and provide only temporary remedies. Commodity loans are quickly disbursable and are not tied to specific projects. This allows great flexibility in the use of these funds, and recipients have few restrictions on their use. The Japanese wanted to avoid a misunderstanding of their intentions should the Koreans have transferred these credits to defense purposes, according to a government official involved in these negotiations.[43]

The Chun-Nakasone joint communiqué made no mention of the specific amount of the economic cooperation agreement. It contained, instead, a vague Japanese commitment to "cooperate to the extent possible" (*kanno na kagiri kyoryoku o okonau*).[44] A month and a half later, Foreign Minister Abe Shintaro seemed to call the $4 billion commitment into question before the Diet Budget Committee. He stated that the $4 billion was not a promise but an intention. Korean aid project proposals are still being assessed and evaluated, he explained, so the government remains uncertain if changes in the amount will need to be made. The $4 billion, he continued, is a rough approximation of the amount Japan expects to provide. He concluded optimistically that the current prospects appear to favor the attainment of that amount.[45] According to a Korean Embassy spokesperson, "We see it as a commitment" and not an intention.[46]

The joint communiqué also avoided a strong condemnation of North Korea. The South Korean side preferred a "threat from the north" clause in the communiqué, but the Japanese refused. Nakasone emphasized instead his support for a resumption of unification talks between Seoul and Pyongyang. After his return, the cabinet indicated its favorable attitude toward "cross recognition," a formula whereby the United States and Japan would recognize Pyongyang if the Soviet Union and China recognize Seoul. Foreign Minister Abe asserted before the Budget Committee that the Nakasone cabinet does not consider North Korea a threat and expressed hopes for private exchanges with the north that would create an environment favorable for a North-South dialogue.[47]

The South Korean side announced that Chun and Nakasone, in their private meetings, agreed to strengthen security cooperation between Japan, Korea, and the United States. The Japanese side immediately denied such an agreement. At a press conference Nakasone maintained that he had informed Chun that Japan could not cooperate militarily because of constitutional restrictions. The joint communiqué contained a clause that Japan recognized that peace and stability on the Korean peninsula is vital to Japan and the entire Asian region. This statement differed little from the various Korea clauses found in U.S.-Japan joint communiqués since the Richard Nixon-Sato Eisaku communiqué of 1969.[48]

How should one view Japanese aid to Korea? Japanese explanations are far from clear. The official explanation in 1983 divorces Korean aid from comprehensive security and stresses interdependence considerations. Why did Japan hesitate in placing Korea within the comprehensive security framework? Officials assert that Chun's aid demand confronted the government at a time when Suzuki had just adopted comprehensive security as national policy but had not yet consolidated the concept or considered practical policy measures. "Korea's challenge provoked a fear that comprehensive security as a concept would have been destroyed. It had already reached its limit at that time," according to one source.[49] This response ignores the fact that strategic aid flowed to Turkey, Pakistan, Thailand, Egypt, and China for political-strategic reasons in the absence of comprehensive security rationales.

The LDP's official position clearly distinguishes between comprehensive security and interdependence. Interdependence is a broad concept, according to a party position statement, that includes geographic, historical, political, and economic aspects. The focus of comprehensive security, on the other hand, is too narrow; therefore, economic cooperation only for Korea's defense and security efforts is not possible. The focus of Japan's aid policy, the report notes, must remain economic development and the people's livelihood within the broader framework of interdependence and humanitarian aid.[50]

Privately, however, many government officials unhesitatingly link Korean aid to comprehensive security. Some state outright that aid to Korea is Japanese strategic assistance, though not in the Korean sense of direct contributions to defense spending and a military buildup. Today the nervousness over aid to Korea has subsided somewhat as the government decided that it fits comfortably within Suzuki's category of "areas which are important to the maintenance of peace and stability of the world."[51] But, ultimately, Japanese officials prefer to stress that Korea is a unique case in economic assistance policy.

The confusion in defining the role of economic aid to Korea in overall Japanese security policy reflects the existence of domestic limits on Nakasone's assertive diplomacy. The economic aid to Korea is based on strategic reasons, but the official rationale must remain pacific. Both Ohira and Suzuki could live with this "neither fish nor fowl" public image of the Korean aid outcome under Nakasone. But the fact that both hawks and doves must soar through the clouds of caution also indicates that the sky is not the limit but has its limits.

Notes

1. *Asahi Shimbun,* May 12, 1983; and Japan, Ministry of Foreign Affairs, Economic Cooperation Bureau, "Japan's Economic Cooperation," February 1, 1982, p. 8.

2. Japan, Ministry of Foreign Affairs, *Diplomatic Bluebook 1981 Edition: Review of Recent Developments in Japan's Foreign Relations* (Tokyo: Foreign Press Center/Japan, 1981), pp. 66–7.

3. Ibid., p. 67.

4. *Asian Wall Street Journal,* May 5, 1978.

5. Japan, Ministry of Foreign Affairs, Economic Cooperation Bureau, *Keizai Kyoryoku ni Kansuru Kihon Shiryo,* February 1983, p. 27.

6. See tables in Alan Rix, *Japan's Economic Aid* (New York: St. Martin's Press, 1980), p. 223, and ibid., p. 26.

7. *New York Times,* March 24, 1981.

8. Ibid.

9. Ibid., June 26, 1981.

10. Shumitsu Miyazawa and Shigemi Katabami, "Economic Cooperation with Thailand and the Philippines: Nakasone's Visit Strengthens Bonds," *Look Japan,* July 10, 1983, p. 14.

11. Ministry of Foreign Affairs, "Kihon Shiryo," p. 27.

12. See chart in William L. Brooks and Robert M. Orr, Jr., "Japan's Foreign Economic Assistance," *Asian Survey* 25(March 1985):330.

13. Koichiro Matsuura, "Sogo Anzen Hosho Seisaku toshite no Keizai Kyoryoku," address delivered before the Sogo Anzen Chosakai, Dai Yon-kai Kenkyukai, April 4, 1981, p. 10.

14. Interview, February 16, 1983.

15. Interview, July 27, 1982.

16. *New York Times,* December 3, 1981.

17. Matsuura, "Sogo Anzen Seisaku," pp. 7–8.

18. Quoted in Research Institute for Peace and Security, *Asian Security 1982* (Tokyo: Nikkei Business Publishing Company, 1982), p. 151.

19. Kenichi Yanagi, "Japan's Economic Cooperation Taking a New Direction," *Japan Times,* September 29, 1981.

20. Ibid., and Koichiro Matsuura, "Japan's Role in International Cooperation," *National Development* (September 1981): 64.

21. Martin E. Weinstein, "Japan's Defense Policy and the May 1981 Summit," *Journal of Northeast Asian Studies* (March 1982): 26.

22. Ibid., p. 27.

23. Ibid.

24. Research Institute for Peace and Security, *Asian Security 1982,* p. 151.

25. Text found in *New York Times,* May 9, 1981.

26. Ibid.

27. Ibid. It also stated that the two leaders "will continue to assist the victims of international instability through their aid to Indochinese, Afghan and African refugees."

28. Shigekazu Matsumoto, "Progress and Policy Formulation of Japan's External Assistance," paper delivered at "The U.S. Congress and the Japanese: Conference on Comparative Studies in Foreign Policy," Honolulu, February 9–12, 1983, p. 12.

29. Keiko Atsumi, "Japan Is No Exception to World Wide Trend of Declining Development Assistance," *Industrial Review of Japan 1983,* p. 20.

30. Research Institute for Peace and Security, *Asian Security 1982,* p. 151.

31. See the study by Hong N. Kim, "Politics of Japan's Economic Aid to South Korea," *Asia Pacific Community* (Spring 1983):80–102.

32. The Japanese media covered the aid issue and Nakasone's visit to Seoul extensively. These points were culled from newspapers and journal articles and from interviews in Tokyo during the author's stay from September 1982 to August 1983.

33. Kim, "South Korea," p. 81.

34. Atsumi, "No Exception," p. 20.

35. For example, see his Kuala Lumpur speech, *Japan Times,* May 10, 1983, and *Mainichi Daily News,* May 10, 1983. See also *Nihon Keizai Shimbun,* May 6, 1983, and *Yomiuri Shimbun,* May 9, 1983, for this theme in other ASEAN countries.

36. *Asahi Shimbun,* January 2, 1984.

37. For example, see the January 6, 1984 *Asahi Shimbun* interview with Director General Kurihara Yuko.

38. Yasuhiro Nakasone, "Toward Comprehensive Security," *Japan Echo* 5, no. 4(1978):34 and 36.

39. Ibid., p. 36.

40. Ibid., p. 39.

41. For the text in English, see *Japan Times,* December 4, 1982.

42. The Japanese mass media reported extensively the various details of each side's negotiating positions, but the image persists that the Koreans emerged victorious from the entire aid episode. This may be attributed to the fact that even the $4 billion of $6 billion is not that bad a prize, and that while Japan may have done well on economic aspects, the Chun government reaped great benefits politically and diplomatically.

43. Interview, March 16, 1983.

44. See *Nihon Keizai Shimbun,* January 13, 1983.

45. *Asahi Shimbun,* March 4, 1983.

46. Interview, April 6, 1983.

47. *Asahi Shimbun,* March 4, 1983.

48. *Asahi Evening News,* January 13, 1983.

49. Interview, December 16, 1982.

50. Liberal Democratic Party, Policy Affairs Research Council, Special Committee on Overseas Economic Cooperation, *Waga To no Keizai Kyoryoku Seisaku ni Tsuite* (Tokyo: Jiyu Minshuto Seimu Chosakai, 1982), pp. 116-7.

51. Koichiro Matsuura, "'Keizai Kyoryoku Taikoku Nihon' e no Michi," *Keizai to Gaiko* (March 1982):23.

4

The Limits of Strategic Aid: Aid and Ambiguity

> We don't want them to define it [strategic aid]. Once we start talking about it, the media and opposition parties will rise to hurt the government. ... It's like the story of Americans who went to Japan before Perry. The Japanese refused to deal with them on a regularized basis, so the Americans ran up the Dutch flag and business went on as usual.
> —An American aid official

> The fuzziness comes from the top.
> —An American government official

The conceptualization, justification, and implementation of Japan's strategic aid policy have been confusing and often tortured. The policy has zigzagged its way to rapid expansion, however, within the past decade. The past three cabinets—of Ohira Masayoshi, Suzuki Zenko, and Nakasone Yasuhiro—have all endorsed and promoted strategic and political uses of aid in their own way, regardless of the conceptual rubrics used to justify or disguise it. Whatever the guise, strategic aid has established a solid footing in Japanese foreign policy. But in view of conceptual uncertainties and fluctuations, questions arise concerning the extent of the solidity of that footing, given severe domestic challenges to the use of strategic aid, and concerning the potential for the expansion of its scope and size, given the ad hoc method of its birth and the selective expansion beyond the confines of Asia.

The government's calibration of ambiguity in policy explanations enabled strategic aid to survive and assume a significant role in Japanese foreign policy. In that sense the domestic footing appears solid. However, the government remains exceedingly sensitive to the climate of unease toward security-related issues. Its greatest fear is the dissipation of the broad consensus on economic cooperation, and this ensures a cautious and truncated case-by-case development of the strategic aid component in the near future. For the government recognizes that the aid consensus is actually softer than most observers assume.

In addition to the political climate, strategic aid policy faces obstacles posed by technical problems involving the budget, the policy process, and the nature of Japanese aid itself. ODA has been tailored to achieve specific economic objectives throughout the postwar years; therefore, the existing types of aid and the policy mechanism make it difficult to deal effectively with immediate, direct political-security requirements in a convincing fashion. The government's difficulty in achieving the aid-doubling goal may also portend the onset of greater caution in making future international aid commitments.

Selling Aid

Strategic aid both responds to and anticipates the wishes of the Japanese people. It responds to a realization that Japan has a responsibility to contribute to international society, including greater attention to security affairs. It anticipates their wish to contribute in a nonmilitary manner, relying instead on the use of the nation's economic capabilities. Defense matters have been openly debated in Japan since the mid-1970s, and the populace has gradually come to accept the SDF and the U.S.-Japan Security Treaty. While recognizing the need to exert greater efforts in the defense field, the people remain reluctant to build up the SDF or increase defense spending beyond the 1 percent of GNP mark, established as national policy in 1976 by the Miki Takeo cabinet. The majority of the people support either the status quo or a slight increase in defense capabilities.[1]

The popularity of comprehensive security rests on the public's assumption that the concept stresses nonmilitary security approaches, especially economic diplomatic tools. However, the public recoils from the politicization of economic policy, including aid, which one analyst dubs "politophobia."[2] This accounts for the resort by the government to several confusing concepts and "philosophies" to justify aid policy.

Until 1973 the government kept secret the exact amounts of aid to specific countries on the grounds that disclosure would prompt complaints from recipients who received less than others. The Foreign Ministry changed this policy in 1977, after widespread questioning of a grant for a high school in Korean President Park Chung Hee's home province.[3] Since that time the MFA has devoted considerable efforts to publicize the benefits of aid to the nation. As the director of the Economic Cooperation Bureau noted in 1983, "In order to expand aid under the current severe fiscal constraints, we need to conduct public relations activities to deepen understanding and generate support from the people for the importance of aid. These activities have not been fully effective in the past and should be strengthened in the future."[4]

The publication of the Foreign Ministry's *Keizai Kyoryoku no Rinen— Seifu Kaihatsu Enjo wa Naze Okonau no ka* (The Philosophy of Economic Cooperation—Why Give Official Development Assistance?) marked a major public relations effort to explain and "sell" aid to the people. It was intended for domestic consumption and was not translated into English. The Foreign ministry also conducted its first evaluation of aid projects and published the findings in 1982. The objective was to convince the public that their taxes were being used abroad effectively (in 98 selected projects in 21 countries).[5] The findings of the report were "made public in the earnest hope that it would deepen the understanding of the people on aid problems."[6]

The Ministry of International Trade and Industry (MITI) publishes an annual white paper on economic cooperation, *Keizai Kyoryoku no Genjo to Mondaiten* (The Present Situation and Problems of Economic Coopera-tion). The authors designed the 1981 edition to respond directly to the concern among officials about the lack of knowledge among the people about the importance of aid. The aid philosophy formed the central focus of that issue. Some MITI officials argue within the ministry that the white paper should be shortened and the writing simplified in order to attract a wider audience. They argue, so far to no avail, that the ministry must counter charges that the white paper is written for use by Japanese businesses with overseas operations in developing nations.[7]

In 1985 it was the Foreign Ministry that acted to shorten and simplify the MITI white paper—in English. This report, *Japan's Official Development Assistance 1984 Annual Report,* represented the first official aid annual report in English and indicated the Foreign Ministry's sensitivity to foreign assessments of Japan's aid policy. The compact volume modified the 1984 issue of MITI's *Keizai Kyoryoku no Genjo to Mondaiten* and included the country-by-country charts and statistics for aid performance in 1983. Inter-estingly for the foreign audience, the political rationale for aid policy per-vades the introductory sections in a way it is downplayed in Japanese language publications on aid. "Aid for peace and stability" is stressed, and a short section on public opinion reports that a majority of the Japanese people favor the use of aid for political purposes.[8] The straightforward and confident assertion of popular support for political aid, however, masks the underlying unease within the ministry about the people's understand-ing of aid policy and tolerance for strategically inclined economic assistance.

The gap between policy explanations and actual policy disturbs many policymakers. Foreign Ministry officials lament the practical need for the "tail wagging the dog" approach, as one official puts it, and hope for a narrowing of the gap between rhetoric and substance at some point in time. But they remain resigned to this approach as long as they feel insecure about the depth of public support for economic cooperation.[9] A 1982 poll indicated that 37 percent of the people support the aid-doubling program even if sacrifices had to be made at home, while 27 percent favored a reduction in aid because of budget cutbacks in social welfare spending.[10] A Finance Ministry official cited another, and perhaps a more ominous, poll showing 40 percent in favor of aid despite sacrifices but with 36 percent opposed.[11]

The government, and especially the aid bureaucrats, would feel hesitant to risk a loss of domestic support for overall economic aid policy by openly and strongly expanding strategic aid. Prime Minister Nakasone reflects this cautious approach. "I'll decide defense and ODA spending," he once stated resolutely, only to change his tone later in reference to aid: "The effective use of the people's taxes is important."[12]

Conditional Consensus

The Japanese Diet's interest in aid is a recent phenomenon, sparked by the Korean aid demand, the sixth replenishment of the International Development Association (IDA, the soft loan window of the World Bank), the apparent globalization and strategic content of aid and humanitarian obligations to poor nations.[13] Heightened interest, according to one bureaucrat, does not translate into influence on policy: "Opposition parties have no influence whatsoever, except to say that Japan must give aid to the developing nations. They all agree on that."[14] An opposition party member basically concurs: "The LDP controls the money and the bureaucrats decide policy. The opposition politicians then look at each country's needs, watch out for the enrichment of the wealthy classes (in recipient nations) and make sure money goes to education and so forth."[15]

The opposition parties join the ruling LDP each year in approving hefty increases in the economic cooperation budget without protest. This has not always been the case, for the Japan Socialist Party (JSP) and the Japan Communist Party (JCP) in particular vehemently berated the government during the Vietnam War era as a surrogate for the United States. While the United States poured troops and material into South Vietnam, they charged, Japan propped up U.S. puppets through the extension of economic aid. They also questioned foreign aid for foreigners at that time, arguing that money should flow instead to rural and local regions, an argument that weakened as the Japanese economy strengthened.[16]

"The opposition parties are trying to bury the past," commented a long-time LDP aid expert with some bitterness, noting that the LDP faced a constant battle with the left-wing opposition parties on any aid decision.[17]

Those confrontational days seem past, with one journalist implying that the LDP "bought off" the opposition: "An expansion of her export markets and the securing of a steady supply of energy and natural resources. Put another way, it was because of this promise of reward to Japan as a whole that the opposition parties were easily persuaded to go along with the LDP's basic strategy for foreign aid."[18]

All opposition parties share a common preference for and emphasis on the humanitarian and peaceful objectives and uses of aid. The JSP prefers humanitarian and multilateral aid devoid of political coloring. The JCP approves of humanitarian and interdependence rationales as long as Japanese aid does not serve a surrogate role for "U.S. imperialism's world strategy."[19] The Clean Government Party (Komeito) holds that the real road to world peace lay through the solution of the North-South problem; nations should reject military assistance and the United Nations should be the focus of Japan's multilateral assistance and Asia the focus of bilateral assistance.[20] The Democratic Socialist Party (DSP) has become active on North-South issues in recent years, encouraged by its major support group, the Japan Confederation of Labor (Domei), a federation of basically private enterprise unions in Japanese firms heavily engaged in international trade, including commercial relations with the developing nations.[21]

Since the start of the defense debate in the mid-1970s, all opposition parties have moved closer toward common ground. They favor a less than 1 percent of GNP defense budget and oppose a significant defense buildup. Komeito accepted the constitutionality of the SDF and the necessity for the U.S.-Japan Security Treaty in the early 1980s. The DSP calls for a strong Japanese defense posture. Neither the JSP nor JCP advocate the immediate abrogation of the Security Treaty or the dismantling of the SDF. The new JSP chairperson began espousing a confusing "unconstitutional but legal" formula for the SDF in 1983 and virtually ruled out abrogation of the Security Treaty (by leaving the decision in U.S. hands).[22] But a more forthright stance on the defense issue does not carry over to support for a more forthright economic aid policy that encompasses security considerations.

All opposition parties are united against the use of economic aid for strategic and military purposes. Even the slightest strategic coloring raises eyebrows. For example, opposition parties paid close attention to a $10 million commodity aid agreement with Jamaica, extended by the Suzuki cabinet in response to a Reagan administration request in 1981, and a commodity loan to the Philippines in 1984, when circumstances of opposition leader Benigno Aquino's assassination remained unclear.[23]

The economic aid agreement with Korea occasioned the greatest show of vociferous unanimity among the opposition. The DSP, Komeito, and New Liberal Club welcomed the Nakasone-Chun summit and economic aid to improve the people's welfare, but all three parties unequivocally opposed military and security uses. The JSP called the agreement "de facto military aid" and was joined by the JCP and the United Socialist Democratic Party in denouncing the attempt by the government to create a U.S.-Japan-South Korea "military alliance."[24]

The opposition parties serve as a watchdog against strategic aid. The government prefers to avoid headline-making controversies and walks a tightrope despite the opposition's basic inability to prevent such aid. In the Korean case a Foreign Ministry official acknowledged that the aid to Korea "is strategic aid, but we can't make it explicit for domestic reasons."[25] Another official cited the government's sensitivity to criticism from the opposition: "What is important is to settle the matter in a way that can be explained to the Diet."[26]

The opposition's ability to embarrass and restrict government aid policy is not limited to politicization and publicity tactics. An opposition coalition managed to codify restrictions against military aid in the form of two resolutions by the House of Representatives Foreign Affairs Committee. In April 1978, the resolution urged the government to more than double ODA in five years (later accomplished in three years) and to establish basic principles for economic cooperation, including the following: "The government should take effective measures to forestall any attempt to divert Japan's aid to military purposes or any purpose which would intensify international conflicts." The March 1981 resolution focused on the peaceful intent of aid policy: The government must 1) refrain from extending economic and technical aid that may be utilized for military purposes, including the building of military facilities, and 2) ensure that economic and technical aid to parties engaged in conflicts not intensify those conflicts.[27]

Japanese cabinets have adhered to these injunctions against military purposes on numerous occasions. During Nakasone's ASEAN trip, President Suharto of Indonesia requested industrial technology transfers to aid Indonesia's defense industry, probably influenced by Naskasone's decision in December 1982 to provide military technology to the United States. Nakasone refused the request.[28] Oman requested aid for its coast guard, for search and rescue missions, but the government refrained, fearing difficulties in the Diet if the opposition linked the issue to sea-lane defense.[29] The government acts cautiously even in relatively safe cases if even a slight chance exists that the opposition would call attention to the aid request.

The opposition's ability to focus unwanted publicity on a specific case of economic assistance and the Diet's restrictions on military assistance narrow the parameters of the government's aid policy. The government responds by exposing a dual face on aid policy explanations. To other nations, especially the United States, Japan insists there is no trade-off between aid and defense efforts. Economic assistance policy, the Japanese assert, is not intended to substitute for military preparedness and efforts. To its own people, each cabinet tends to emphasize the appropriateness of the trade-off: Japan will adhere to constitutional restrictions on military defense policy while pursuing an economically oriented peace diplomacy that utilizes such tools as economic assistance. This tenuous political environment puts a premium on the government's ability to camouflage political-security aid with humanitarian, interdependence, or comprehensive security coverings. Any expansion of strategic aid will thus occur gradually and in a manner that retains the ambiguous shading of aid policy.

The government will seek to avoid an open flare-up of controversy on any aid issue, deferring to the opposition insistence on the retention of a pacific, nonbelligerent image of Japanese diplomacy. One significant result of this situation has been an unofficial consensus within political and bureaucratic circles that the annual increase in the economic cooperation budget shall not fall below the annual rate of increase in the defense budget.[30] Over the past years, aid has consistently enjoyed annual increases that exceeded defense increases. In 1983, 1984, and 1985, aid spending was treated as a special case.

One can now understand why the annual aid budget hikes consistently and predictably surpass defense spending increases. It is a political decision designed to placate critics, assure the public, and ensure continued defense increases in an age of austerity. Nothing symbolizes this delicate, interdependent relationship between aid and defense spending more than the tandem announcements of the Third Medium Term ODA program and the new five-year defense plan.

On September 18, 1985 the Nakasone cabinet adopted a defense plan for 1986–1990 that requires approximately 7.9 percent annual budget increases. Based on current estimates, this may carry defense spending above the 1 percent of GNP ceiling established by the Miki Takeo cabinet in 1976. Predictably, opposition parties raised strong objections to the plan. On the very same day, the cabinet announced the third aid doubling plan, pledging to reach an accumulated spending target of $40 billion in seven years. Annual aid budgets require increases of approximately 10.4 percent, thus ensuring that defense budgets do not become the fastest expanding budget item each year.[31] Economic aid increases thus continue to set the pace and make defense increases more respectable and acceptable.

One should not assume that the Liberal Democrats are unhappy with all of this. To think that the LDP would leap headlong into a full-scale strategic aid program if opposition constraints were removed is erroneous. Ohira and Suzuki would have hesitated; Nakasone may have taken moderate steps in that direction but would not have risked widespread popular antagonism, including opposition within the LDP (for another constraint on LDP strategic aid policy is the lack of consensus within the ruling party itself). After all, how could the opposition adopt resolutions against military aid in a Diet and a committee controlled by the numerically superior LDP?

While some LDP members advocate strategic uses of aid, many others sound like the opposition. One aid advocate heatedly denied any relevance to security policy: "There is no strategic motive in Japan's economic cooperation. Absolutely none. It's completely wrong [to think that way]. It is given for humanitarian reasons. Economic cooperation is a means of preventing war. If you are going to shell out for defense, it is also necessary to support economic cooperation. Economic cooperation is cheap."[32]

To the extent LDP factions can be identified with policy positions, the Nakasone, Tanaka Kakuei, and Fukuda Takeo factions retain "hawkish" reputations, while the Komoto Toshio faction (formerly the Miki Takeo faction) and Ohira-Suzuki faction (currently chaired by Miyazawa Kiichi) have a "dovish" cast. The Ohira-Suzuki faction prides itself on representing the conservative mainstream, tracing its factional lineage back to Yoshida Shigeru, the dominant political leader who led the nation through the immediate postwar period. This faction adheres to the basic policy line Yoshida established for postwar Japan: concentration on economic development, maintenance of a limited and minimal self-defense capacity, and reliance on the United States for national security. One analyst pictured Ohira as attempting to break down the taboo in the public mind against open and serious consideration of defense issues while at the same time trying to avoid both defense spending increases and efforts by right-wing factions (Nakasone and Fukuda) to focus exclusively on military security.[33] As one Defense Agency head describes it, "Sometimes a Nakasone current, sometimes an Ohira current. I think this mix within the LDP is healthy."[34]

Factions play only an indirect role in aid policy. Dietmen's leagues, or parliamentary leagues, are cited by aid bureaucrats as wielding more influence. These organizations were formed to promote better relations with specific countries, or nongovernmental organizations (like the Palestine Liberation Organization), but the extent of their actual influence is difficult to determine. The Japan–South Korea Parliamentarians' League, heavily populated with Tanaka and Fukuda faction members, is credited with facilitating the settlement of the aid issue and playing a pivotal role in Nakasone's trip to Seoul.[35]

Within the LDP the Special Committee on Overseas Economic Cooperation, composed of numerous members of the late former LDP Vice President Kawashima Shojiro's faction, actively monitors aid policy through regional, country-specific, and functional task forces. The Special Committee issued a party position on economic aid policy in 1982 that revealed hesitation on Korean aid for security reasons and extended olive branches to Vietnam and Laos.[36] The Special Committee's influence is limited, however, and one should keep in mind that the party position was drafted by the Economic Cooperation Bureau of the Foreign Ministry (except for the chairperson's introduction).

The Bureaucracy and Executive Activism

That the bureaucracy plays a pivotal role in overall economic assistance policy seems only natural. Politicians deal with myriad issues daily, with aid far down on the priority list. Aid policy lacks a solid constituency engaged in active lobbying efforts and produces few votes at the polls. Politicians lack the technical knowledge necessary to assess aid projects and impact. They lack the capacity to gather aid-related information or engage in any kind of sophisticated analysis, given their small personal, Diet committee, and party organ staffs. They also lack the U.S. congressmen's ability to question the amounts and uses of aid to specific countries since the Diet receives a general and not an itemized budget. Nor do they pass aid legislation since Japan lacks Foreign Assistance Legislation like the U.S. Congress. Diet members' principal function entails the passage of the gross figures of the annual aid budget. And bilateral aid agreements are considered administrative agreements, which are not subject to formal Diet approval.[37]

The bureaucracy, on the other hand, is well equipped to deal with aid policy. The various ministries that oversee aid contain bureaus and sections specifically assigned to aid activities. They continually train and nurture their own aid experts because of the regular rotation of civil servants within the ministries. They are able to follow aid developments on a daily basis. Bureaucrats possess information-gathering and analysis capabilities, and they are the ones who brief politicians and initiate the aid process to specific recipients and projects. Economic cooperation budgets are determined each year in the ministries, not in Diet committees. Bureaucrats also implement aid policy. By comparison, politicians are no match for this array of human resources and technical expertise. An LDP Diet member explains,

> The LDP has no unified policy on aid. It is more of a case by case basis. The Special Committee [on Overseas Economic Cooperation] sets up research projects to look into aid to various regions. This is a positive development, but the Foreign Ministry basically has a free hand in policy. It does what it wants. It hasn't reached a stage yet where Foreign Ministry people are called in and the Committee tells them what it wants. It is more of a report after the fact, that aid was given to country X.[38]

Aid bureaucrats refer to a time when politicians did have a strong say in aid matters. Former LDP Vice President Kawashima is frequently cited for his efforts on behalf of aid to Indonesia.[39] Those days are gone, say these officials; parliamentary leagues have replaced these individuals.

The aid bureaucracy is not monolithic, however. The Foreign Ministry serves as the acknowledged window of foreign aid policy. It maintains a large, active Economic Cooperation Bureau to oversee most aspects of bilateral and multilateral assistance. The MFA also serves as the formal diplomatic window to the rest of the world since it is the principal guardian of Japan's foreign relations. Theoretically, it is in the best position to integrate aid into overall foreign policy. In reality Japan's aid policy-making process is decentralized and ponderous.

Jurisdiction for each component of aid policy is dispersed throughout the administrative branch of government, often with overlapping responsibilities. Multilateral aid is divided between the foreign affairs and finance ministries. The Ministry of Foreign Affairs handles UN-related aid, and the Ministry of Finance (MOF) oversees contributions to the multilateral development banks; both deal with the OECD's Development Assistance Committee. The MFA oversees bilateral grants and refugee aid; MITI supervises yen loans; the MOF stands as the holder of the purse strings for the aid budget; and the Economic Planning Agency ostensibly coordinates overall aid policy. These institutions constitute the four pillars of the aid bureaucracy. Their aid officials meet periodically in joint meetings *(yon-shocho kaigi)*, where aid policy is formally decided. In addition the MFA's Japan International Cooperation Agency administers technical assistance, including Japan's version of the U.S. Peace Corps, and the Economic Planning Agency's Overseas Economic Cooperation Fund (OECF) administers yen loan projects. And when the need arises, other ministries and institutions are called in, especially the Export Import Bank and the ministries of transportation, construction, health and welfare, and agriculture, forestries, and fisheries. The aid apparatus and the policy process have been well studied elsewhere and need not be repeated here,[40] except to note that this state of affairs also affects strategic aid policy.

The Foreign Ministry is most conscious of the political and diplomatic impact and implications of economic assistance; it serves as the command post for strategic uses of aid. And it is the strongest proponent of comprehensive national security within the bureaucracy. It must struggle, however, not only with a skeptical opposition but also against apathy among other aid bureaucrats. Other ministries have revealed a singular lack of enthusiasm for comprehensive security and strategic assistance. When queried about the relevance of comprehensive security and strategic considerations in specific aid decisions, MITI, MOF, and OECF officials assert that these aspects lie outside their jurisdiction. These aspects are left to Foreign Ministry officials in aid meetings; others do not raise the issues.

"Political considerations are the Foreign Ministry's responsibility," according to a MITI official. "MITI is concerned with economic aspects, with resources, with energy. We don't go so far as to oppose [political considerations], but we do leave them to the Foreign Ministry and the prime minister." Another MITI member noted that "there is a tendency in MITI to counterbalance any major theme of the moment." When comprehensive security appeared too dominant an approach to aid in the early 1980s, this official relates, MITI balanced its visibility by downplaying it in its economic cooperation white paper.[41]

An LDP politician who favors greater political criteria in determining aid policy places the blame for Japanese aid's "economic animal" image squarely on MITI's shoulders:

> The Finance Ministry's role is understandable. It's all right for them to focus on financial aspects. That's its job. The problem is MITI. MITI has always viewed aid as a means of benefiting Japanese companies, and this thinking still remains. Strategic thinking hasn't penetrated that ministry. The Foreign Ministry should take the lead on aid since it views economic cooperation from a wider, more international perspective.[42]

The MFA faces a difficult situation on strategic aid, forced to maintain the popular consensus on economic aid and to seek ministerial consensus on specific uses of strategic aid. The Foreign Ministry's power over domestic policy is limited, and its influence over other ministries is restricted by the dispersed nature of aid and aid-policy-making procedures. Its position and policy stances are not bolstered by a strong strategic aid lobby urging the government to abandon its economics-first aid policy approach. Strategic aid has had basically one consistent source of support outside the Foreign Ministry—the prime minister and cabinet. Without the support of the prime minister in particular, the MFA could not have come as far as it has with comprehensive security or strategic aid.

The Ohira, Suzuki, and Nakasone cabinets have either initiated or endorsed the use of economic aid as a diplomatic tool. They have not only legitimized strategic aid within the bureaucracy, under whatever slogan or concepts used at the moment, but also provided the foreign policy framework for aid policy: to contribute to international society as a member of the West beyond purely economic efforts.

Ohira initiated aid to "countries bordering areas of conflict," the Vietnam aid freeze, and the first ODA to China. One view holds that the MFA and MOF showed a negative attitude on aid to Turkey despite the West German request because Japan had been snubbed by the United States and West Europeans at the Guadelope summit (Japan was not invited to attend). Ohira is said to have pushed it through despite this opposition from the bureaucrats.[43]

Suzuki exhibited caution toward the blatant, open use of aid for strategic purposes, but he did adopt comprehensive security as national policy, created the new Ministerial Council on Comprehensive Security and initiated the New Medium Term Target for doubling aid in five years. Despite the hesitancy on aid to South Korea, aid to non-Asian strategic countries increased under his administration, and he held firm on the aid freeze to Vietnam.

Nakasone has stayed the course, endorsing comprehensive security and exhibiting a positive attitude toward the use of economic aid as a diplomatic tool. The South Korean aid issue is the most visible example of Nakasone's orientation, but his cabinet has maintained the general momentum of strategic aid that developed under Ohira and Suzuki, which will be discussed in the following chapter.

These examples illustrate the ability of political leaders to transcend the bureaucracy's basically slow, jurisdiction-conscious, cautious, and incremental tendencies. The cabinet sets the framework for policy and creates momentum within the bureaucracy. In this sense, the Foreign Ministry reinforces cabinet policy guidelines. The problem, however, is the sporadic nature of cabinet and prime ministerial involvement. They participate actively when they become concerned over specific countries or pet policies. If cabinet momentum falters, policy falters, as seen in the abandonment of the "countries bordering areas of conflict" initiative and comprehensive national security until its revival (perhaps temporary) under Nakasone. Since cabinets tend to harbor doubts about openly pursuing an extensive strategic aid policy, and since the MFA is sensitive to the public mood and interministerial harmony, the government may not seek a rapid expansion of strategic aid's scope or pace in the near future.

Aid Disbursement

Several practical problems also pose difficulties in expanding strategic assistance. First, Japanese aid policy is reactive, responding to specific requests by recipient governments *(yosei-shugi)*. Japanese economic assistance is basically project aid. The Japanese hesitate in providing aid for unclear purposes, a problem with the South Korean aid demand early in the negotiation process; they are more comfortable with specific projects. In 1982 project loans totaled 87.1 percent of Japanese yen loans, while commodity aid comprised 12.9 percent.[44] If aid is to expand rapidly and substantially, the government must find larger numbers of projects. This is difficult given the reactive nature of aid policy and given the current emphasis on effectiveness and the need for suitable, feasible projects. Aid expansion may be limited by the recipient nation's absorptive capacity.

The reactive nature of aid policy gives rise to another problem: the origins of recipient nations' aid proposals. The Japanese government's aid personnel is limited in number and ability to seek out projects. Unlike the U.S. Agency for International Development, the Japanese cannot maintain an extensive network of aid missions in developing countries to seek and monitor suitable aid projects. Aid requests are initially received and processed by Japanese embassies. They must await aid application forms from the other party, and the Japanese do not have much confidence in the recipient governments' abilities to adequately find, develop, and propose aid projects. Each year the OECF invites government officials from recipient nations to Tokyo to learn how to properly formulate and prepare aid request forms.

Who fills the gap between inadequate capabilities on both the donor and recipient sides? The source for almost all project proposals for yen loans from developing countries is overseas branches of Japanese business firms. This is where the business community's involvement in aid policy begins. In contrast to bureaucrats stationed in an embassy for one or two years, Japanese firms are staffed by experts familiar with local languages, cultures, customs, and the political and economic situation. "The bureaucrats are useless," complains a business representative. "They just get in the way."[45]

These Japanese firms seek, find, evaluate, and propose aid projects. They often assist in the writing of the official proposals submitted to Japanese embassies by various recipient government agencies. Once submitted, these firms lobby in Tokyo through their home offices for the project in the halls of MITI. "Almost all *(hotondo)* yen loan project proposals come from Japanese firms," according to a MITI aid official.[46]

The business community does influence aid policy, but its influence is restricted primarily to specific yen loan projects. It does not determine the overall framework for Japanese aid policy; that remains in the hands of others. For example, the business community is dissatisfied with the government's emphasis on basic human needs since 1981. There is little profit to be made in projects dealing with basic human needs. "The introduction of the basic human needs approach to Japan's aid programs has ushered out the era of ODA-funded large-scale industrial projects," according to one study. "Such projects were judged to benefit only a few in the host country and to accentuate the gap between the rich and the poor."[47] The government seemed influenced also by the spectacular failures of several large-scale projects in ASEAN countries, China and Iran. Policymakers decided that these types of projects should rely on commercial funding sources, but big business would prefer that the government return to the old formula of support for large-scale projects.[48]

Although the government is exerting some efforts to reduce overdependence on project aid,[49] current practices make it exceedingly difficult to argue that aid is extended for strategic rather than economic purposes. Aid, whatever the official rationale, still flows to infrastructure; agriculture, fisheries, and forestry; and mining and manufacturing. (In 1982, 76.4 percent of yen loans went to infrastructure, 12.5 percent to agriculture, fisheries, and forestry, and 10.8 percent to mining and manufacturing.[50])

Table 4-1
Comparison of U.S. and Japanese Aid Forms
(Bilateral Aid)

United States[a]	Japan[b]
I. Economic and financial assistance	I. Economic assistance
A. Development assistance	A. Bilateral grants
B. Public Law 480 (Food for Peace)	1. Economic development assist-
C. Refugee assistance	ance
D. Narcotic control assistance	2. Food aid (Kennedy Round)
E. Inter-American Foundation	3. Aid for increased food produc-
F. Peace Corps	tion
	B. Technical assistance
	1. Acceptance of trainees
	2. Dispatch of personnel
	a. Dispatch of experts
	b. Dispatch of development
	survey teams
	c. Dispatch of Japan Overseas
	Cooperation Volunteers
	3. Equipment and materials
	4. Project type cooperation
	C. Bilateral loans
	1. Project loans
	2. Commodity loans
	3. Debt relief
II. Security assistance	II. Security assistance
A. Foreign military sales	(None)
B. Economic Support Fund	
C. Military assistance program	
D. International military education	
and training	
E. Peacekeeping operations	
F. Anti-terrorism assistance	

[a]Compiled from *International Security and Economic Cooperation Program FY 1983* (U.S. Department of State).

[b]Compiled from *A Guide to Japan's Aid* (1982) and *The Developing Countries and Japan* (1981), both published by the Association for the Promotion of International Cooperation.

The ambiguity of Japan's strategic aid policy is compounded by the lack of any clearly identifiable "security aid" forms. The Japanese walk on one leg in comparison with the United States, which utilizes a wide range of economic, security-related, and military assistance. (See table 4-1.) Even multilateral aid is justified before Congress in security terms, the administration arguing that the major recipients of multilateral development bank funds happen to be American allies or friends, or nations important to U.S. security interests.

Japanese aid types are overwhelmingly economic in nature and purpose. Japan cannot extend military assistance because of Diet restrictions and other practical, nonlegal political constraints. The economic nature of aid forms is advantageous domestically, but should strategic aid expand, foreign proponents may be troubled by the apparent schizophrenic nature of aid policy, while domestic critics will charge that strategic criteria will taint economic aid.

If the government wishes to expand strategic aid, it will rely on two major, less-than-convincing arguments, given the current nature of aid forms: rapid increases in the amount of aid to specific countries and the government's say-so that it is for strategic purposes. The government's say-so may not satisfy many critics, and the amounts may increase but only for the standard uses in the traditional sectors (especially infrastructure). Besides, the amount increases may be exceedingly difficult judging by the record of the New Medium Term Target.

The Unfulfilled Promise

The five-year aid-doubling plan has been plagued by austere annual budgets, a weakened yen, and fluctuations in multilateral aid. When the Suzuki cabinet pledged aid-doubling, it envisioned projected annual increases in the economic cooperation budget of a modest 8.7 percent. Confidence ran high since the previous doubling pledge had been accomplished in three years. In 1977 Tokyo disbursed $1.4 billion, reached $3.3 billion in 1980, and foresaw $5.1 billion at the end of the New Medium Term Target. Aggregate aid disbursement during the last half of the 1970s reached $10.7 billion, which served as the base for the new Target's goal of $21.4 billion. Japan's aid commitments are calculated in dollars, and the government anticipated a continued appreciation of the yen against the dollar, which stood at 220 yen to the dollar when the doubling was pledged.[51]

Misfortune befell the plan immediately. In 1981, the first year of the doubling plan, ODA *decreased* 4.1 percent, to $3.17 billion. In 1982 ODA suffered yet another setback, decreasing 4.7 percent, to $3.02 billion. Contrary to expectations, the yen had depreciated 13 percent immediately, hitting a low of 270 yen to the dollar in two years.[52] Also, multilateral aid dropped in 1982 by a stunning 28 percent from the previous year ($547.5 million) because of difficulties in negotiations for the sixth replenishment of IDA. (On a yen basis multilateral aid dropped 19 percent and overall ODA actually increased 7.7 percent because of an 18 percent rise in bilateral grants and loans; but Japan calculated aid performance in dollars rather than yen.[53])

By 1983 the back-to-back setbacks in the 1981 and 1982 aid condemned the Japanese to playing catch-up, with a need to disburse aid increases of 28.5 percent in each remaining year in order to fulfill its international commitment. This would require large increases in the economic cooperation budget, but the inaugural year of the aid-doubling plan also coincided with the first year of the stringent budget austerity policy that has continued throughout the Suzuki and Nakasone cabinets. While the economic cooperation budget still enjoyed double-digit increases in 1981 (12.8%) and 1982 (11.4%), recent increases proved inadequate to make up the distance lost early in the doubling quest (8.9% in 1983, 9.7% in 1984, and 10% in 1985) even though the government exempted aid from the zero-growth budget guidelines.[54] The 10 percent budget increase in 1985 ensured the failure of the government to fulfill its aid pledge since an increase of 64 percent was required.[55]

The 1983 record confirms the impact of multilateral aid on overall ODA disbursements. The yen had stabilized and ODA leaped 24.4 percent to $3.76 billion because of a 103.6 percent leap in multilateral aid, the result of the settlement of IDA VI and a general capital increase agreement by the Asian Development Bank. At that point fulfillment of the aid-doubling pledge still required a 31.3 percent increase in each of the last two years. In 1984 Japan disbursed a record $4.3 billion in aid, a 15 percent rise from 1983. However, once again, multilateral aid accounted for the increase, leaping 58 percent while bilateral aid disbursements remained at roughly the 1983 level.[56]

The Nakasone cabinet discussed possible modifications of the New Medium Term Target in 1983. Two options that appeared possible were to double only the bilateral component of ODA in view of the wild fluctuations in multilateral aid, or to extend the deadline for doubling by one year, to 1987.[57] Both options would have violated the original spirit and intent of the doubling pledge and would have been a blow to Japan's national prestige; these options were not adopted. The admission of failure at that stage would have been an embarrassment to a nation that contemplates an international role as an aid great power—especially when the starting point for the aid-doubling policy was so modest. The first aid-doubling plan from 1978 to 1980 was accomplished with annual increases of 55.5, 19.1, and 25.3 percent.[58] In 1980 Japan ranked fourteenth in terms of ODA as a percentage of GNP, at 0.32 percent. The figures for the following years were hardly

Table 4–2
Annual ODA Disbursement Totals
(*$ billions*)

Year	Amount	Percentage of GNP
1976	1.10	0.20
1977	1.42	0.21
1978	2.22	0.23
1979	2.64	0.26
1980	3.30	0.32
1981	3.17	0.28
1982	3.02	0.29
1983	3.76	0.33
1984	4.32	0.35

Sources: Ministry of Foreign Affairs, Economic Cooperation Bureau, "Japanese Economic Cooperation" (February 1, 1982); *Japan Times*, July 17, 1983 and June 4, 1983 and January 7, 1984; *Asahi Shimbun*, July 4, 1983; and *Yomiuri Shimbun*, June 9, 1985.

Table 4-3
Official Development Assistance of DAC Countries, 1982-1983
($ millions)

Rank[a]	Country	1983 Amount	1983 Percentage of GNP	1982 Amount	1982 Percentage of GNP	Percentage Change 1982-1983
1	Norway	$ 584	1.06	$ 559	0.99	4.5
2	Netherlands	1,195	0.91	1,472	1.08	-18.8
3	Sweden	799	0.88	987	1.02	-21.1
4	France[b]	3,915	0.76	4,034	0.75	-3.0
5	Denmark	394	0.72	415	0.76	-5.1
6	Belgium	477	0.59	499	0.59	-4.4
7	Australia	753	0.49	822	0.57	-14.6
8	West Germany	3,181	0.49	3,152	0.48	0.9
9	Canada	1,429	0.45	1,197	0.41	19.4
10	United Kingdom	1,601	0.35	1,800	0.37	-11.1
11	Finland	153	0.33	145	0.30	5.5
12	Japan	3,761	0.33	3,023	0.28	24.4
13	Switzerland	318	0.31	252	0.25	26.2
14	New Zealand	61	0.29	65	0.28	-6.2
15	United States	7,950	0.24	8,202	0.27	-3.1
16	Italy	826	0.24	811	0.24	1.8
17	Austria	157	0.23	235	0.35	-33.2
DAC Total		27,534	0.36	27,730	0.38	-0.7

Source: Ministry of Foreign Affairs, Economic Cooperation Bureau.
[a]Ranked by ODA as percentage of GNP in 1983.
[b]Includes overseas territories and prefectures.

impressive: 0.28, 0.29, and 0.33 percent in 1983. In 1984 Japan reached a record high of 0.35 percent, still far from the 0.7 percent of GNP target and still slightly below the DAC average of 0.36 percent.[59] (See tables 4-2 and 4-3).

The per capita amount of aid Japan provides as ODA totaled $27 per year, ranking 14 out of 17 among DAC members in 1980, well below the $100 plus figures attained by Norway, Sweden, and Holland in 1981. Tokyo ranked number 16 of 17 in terms of grant element percentage in 1980 and 1981 (at approximately 75 percent, compared with the 90 to 100 percent ratio reached by 13 DAC members).[60] The grant element rose to 80 percent in 1983, but Japan still lags behind other DAC countries, whose average was 91 percent. (See table 4-4).

Table 4-4
Grant Element and Share of Grants

	Grant Element (%) Japan	Grant Element (%) Average of Total DAC	Share of Grants (%) Japan	Share of Grants (%) Average of Total DAC
1980	74.3	89.9	40.0	75.2
1981	75.3	89.6	43.6	75.2
1982	74.2	90.4	39.8	76.9
1983	79.5	91.2	55.2	79.7

Source: *Japan's Official Development Assistance 1984 Annual Report*, p. 6.

The scale of Japan's aid policy calls into question the vaunted hopes of becoming an "aid great power" or "aid superpower." Even if Japan had attained the $21.4 billion target in five years, the amount seems almost trifling compared with the Reagan administration's request to Congress for over $10 billion in military assistance alone in just one year (1983).[61]

Japan did not achieve its aid-doubling pledge. Tokyo fulfilled 67 percent of the $21.4 billion target, or 98 percent if calculated in yen terms.[62] On March 31, 1986 the 1985 fiscal year comes to an end, and with it the New Medium Term international commitment. The Finance Ministry has already signaled that ODA is no longer a sacred cow entitled to special privileges at budget time each year.[63] The cabinet and Foreign Ministry, however, refuse to yield on the ODA policy priority. The Nakasone cabinet adopted a Third Medium Term Target in September 1985 that once again pledges a doubling of aid. This time, the cabinet exhibited greater caution by pledging the doubling in seven rather than five years. A five-year pledge required annual spending increases of about 14.9 percent, a hefty increase given past budget battles. The additional two years will require estimated annual increases of 10.4 percent.

Given the difficulties in meeting the second Medium Term Target, the government may be flirting with another failure to fulfill its international commitment. Double-digit annual increases will be difficult to negotiate given the Finance Ministry's attitude toward spending and given the Nakasone cabinet's commitment to a policy of budget austerity. Also, the same problems that blunted the previous aid-doubling plan remain intact: exchange rate fluctuations, recipient nation absorptive capacities, and extreme fluctuations in multilateral aid requirements.

In recognition of the difficulty in expanding aid beyond current annual levels, the government has recently begun to emphasize aid quality and effectiveness. Ministries have been discussing modifications of existing uses of aid, including less emphasis on project-oriented aid and more attention to commodity aid.[64] The Foreign Ministry has conducted two studies of aid projects in selected recipient nations. The focus on effective uses of aid is a major component of the Third Medium Term Target.

Another impact of greater caution in aid expansion is a closer scrutiny of Japan's aid-distribution pattern. Japan prefers to concentrate on the Asian region. In an era of austerity, this preference has been strengthened in policymakers' minds. This presents another limit on strategic aid since one of its major requirements is globalization.

Notes

1. R. Drifte, "Part Two: Diplomacy," in J.W.M. Chapman, R. Drifte, and I.T.M. Gow, *Japan's Quest for Comprehensive Security: Defence, Diplomacy and*

Dependence (New York: St. Martin's Press, 1982), p. 94: and Japan, Prime Minister's Office, *Waga Kuni no Heiwa to Anzen ni Kansuru Yoron Chosa,* August 1982, pp. 11-13.

2. See Taketsugu Tsurutani, *Japanese Policy and East Asian Security* (New York: Praeger, 1981).

3. Tsuyoshi Yamamoto, *Nihon no Keizai Enjo* (Tokyo: Sanseido, 1978), pp. 56-7.

4. Kenichi Yanagi, "Japan Broadening Its Role in Field of Aid," *Japan Times,* January 8, 1983.

5. Japan, Ministry of Foreign Affairs, Economic Cooperation Bureau, *Keizai Kyoryoku Hyoka Hokokusho,* September 1982.

6. Yanagi, "Broadening," and also, *Daily Yomiuri,* October 8, 1982.

7. Interview with a MITI official, May 20, 1983.

8. Japan, Ministry of Foreign Affairs, *Japan's Official Development Assistance 1984 Annual Report,* 1985, p. 24.

9. Interviews with officials, and Japan, Ministry of Foreign Affairs, "Anzen Hosho no Gunji-men to Hi-Gunji-men (Toku ni, Anzen Hosho Kara Mita Keizai Kyoryoku no Ichizuke)," April 1982.

10. *Asahi Shimbun,* January 5, 1983.

11. Interview, May 11, 1983.

12. *Asahi Shimbun,* January 27, 1984 and May 4, 1984.

13. Interview with a Foreign Ministry official, November 11, 1982.

14. Interview with a government official, July 18, 1983.

15. Interview, May 25, 1983.

16. Interview with an LDP politician, May 23, 1983.

17. Interview, May 20, 1983.

18. Shinsuke Samejima, "Can Japan Steer Its Foreign Aid Policy Clear of Militarism?" *Japan Quarterly* (January-March 1982):34.

19. Interview with a JCP official; and Yoshitaka Ikeda, "Kyuzo suru Keizai Kyoryoku ni wa Nani o Nerau ka," *Akahata Hyoron Tokushuban,* November 16, 1981, p. 16.

20. Interview, May 25, 1983.

21. Interview with a party official, July 26, 1983.

22. *Japan Times Weekly,* March 17, 1984.

23. *Asahi Shimbun,* March 23, 1984.

24. See *Yomiuri Shimbun,* January 10, 1983 and January 13, 1983; *Mainichi Shimbun,* November 13, 1983; and *Asahi Evening News,* January 13, 1983.

25. Interview, March 16, 1983.

26. Interview, November 17, 1982.

27. Samejima, "Militarism," p. 32; and Japan, Ministry of Foreign Affairs, "Japan's Economic Cooperation," February 1, 1982, pp. 17-19.

28. *Asahi Shimbun,* May 12, 1982.

29. Interview with an MFA official, December 16, 1982.

30. Revealed by an MOF official, July 13, 1983.

31. See *Japan Times Weekly,* October 5, 1985 and October 19, 1985.

32. Interview, Masy 20, 1983.

33. Hideo Otake, *Nihon no Boei to Kokunai Seiji* (Tokyo: Sanichi, 1983), pp. 268 and 349.

34. *Asahi Shimbun,* January 6, 1984.

35. See the study by Hong N. Kim, "Politics of Japan's Economic Aid to South Korea," *Asia Pacific Community* (Spring 1983), and newspapers throughout December 1982.

36. Liberal Democratic Party, Policy Affairs Research Council, Special Committee on Overseas Economic Cooperation, *Waga To no Keizai Kyoryoku Seisaku ni Tsuite* (Tokyo: Jiyu Minshuto Seimu Chosakai, 1982).

37. Shuzo Kimura, "The Role of the Diet in Foreign Policy and Defense," in Francis R. Valeo and Charles E. Morrison, eds., *The Japanese Diet and the U.S. Congress* (Boulder, Colo.: Westview Press, 1983), p. 100.

38. Interview, May 23, 1983.

39. For a detailed look at Kawashima's relationship with the Indonesian leadership, see Masashi Nishihara, *The Japanese and Sukarno's Indonesia: Tokyo-Jakarta Relations, 1951–1966* (Honolulu: University of Hawaii Press, 1976).

40. Almost any book on Japanese aid will note the jurisdictions of the various ministries, but in English, Rix provides the most detailed, comprehensive and informative study, in *Japan's Economic Aid* (New York: St. Martin's Press, 1980).

41. Interviews with officials, May 20, 1983 and July 5, 1983.

42. Interview, May 23, 1983.

43. Otake, *Nihon no Boei,* p. 347.

44. "Government Position Behind Yen Loan Extension: A Growing Role of Yen Loans," *Look Japan,* April 10, 1984, pp. 10–11.

45. Interview, June 14, 1983.

46. Interview, July 5, 1983.

47. William L. Brooks and Robert M. Orr, Jr., "Japan's Foreign Economic Assistance," *Asian Survey* 25(March 1985):327.

48. Interview at Keidanren headquarters in Tokyo, June 14, 1983.

49. For details, see *Japan Times,* March 23, 1983; *Asahi Evening News,* March 7, 1983; and *Mainichi Daily News,* June 25, 1983.

50. "Government Position," pp. 10–11.

51. See Koichiro Matsuura, "Saikin no Namboku Mondai no Doko to Nihon no Keizai Kyoryoku," *Keizai to Gaiko* (December 1982):25; and Ministry of Foreign Affairs, "Japan's Economic Cooperation," p. 12.

52. *Japan Times,* July 17, 1983.

53. See *Asahi Shimbun,* June 4, 1983; *Japan Times,* June 4, 1983; and *Japan Times Weekly,* January 7, 1984.

54. *JEI Report,* February 17, 1984.

55. Ibid., June 12, 1985; and *Asahi Shimbun,* January 3, 1985. According to the Asahi account, widespread agreement existed on a double-digit figure. Finance Minister Takeshita Noboru is quoted as saying, "a round figure would be good"— thus a consensus on 10 percent.

56. See *Yomiuri Shimbun,* June 9, 1985; *JEI Report,* June 21, 1985; *Japan Times Weekly,* June 29, 1985; and Charles Smith, "The Aid Dilemma," *Far Eastern Economic Review* (August 30, 1984):64.

57. *Japan Times,* July 5, 1983.

58. *JEI Report,* February 2, 1981; and Ministry of Foreign Affairs, Economic Cooperation Bureau, *Keizai Kyoryoku ni Kansuru Kihon Shiryo,* February 1983, p. 7.

59. *Yomiuri Shimbun,* June 9, 1985; *JEI Report,* June 2, 1985; and *Japan Times Weekly,* June 29, 1985.

60. Ministry of Foreign Affairs, "Kihon Shiryo," pp. 9–10.

61. *Japan Times,* February 6, 1983.

62. *Yomiuri Shimbun,* June 9, 1985.

63. *Asahi Shimbun,* May 26, 1985.

64. See *Japan Times,* March 23, 1983; *Asahi Evening News,* March 7, 1983; and *Mainichi Daily News,* June 25, 1983.

5

The Limits of Strategic Aid:
Globalism versus Regionalism

> It is necessary for Japan to make a positive contribution to enhance
> stability and development in Asia. This must be done not merely to
> accomplish its mission as a member of the international society but
> to ensure its own existence.
>
> —Ito Soichiro, former Director
> General of the Defense Agency

The first oil crisis of 1973–1974 triggered the globalization of aid policy in the 1970s, as Japan's paramount concern was the securing of raw material and energy sources. The continued globalization of economic assistance for political and strategic and not just economic reasons constitutes a distinguishing feature of aid policy in the 1980s. But by the mid-1980s globalization may have reached its limits. The Japanese basically prefer to stay close to home, in Asia. In fact, upon closer examination, strategic assistance had originally been devised as a formula intended for application in the Asia Pacific region, not throughout the world. Therefore obstacles to the expansion of strategic aid lie not only within the domestic political environment but also in the minds of Japanese leaders and policymakers themselves. The leadership in other words is not inclined toward a rapid unleashing of strategic aid far beyond Japan's borders, even at the behest of the United States.

Globalization

Japan's economic assistance policy commenced in the 1950s with war reparation and economic cooperation agreements with Asian countries Japan had occupied during World War II. During the 1950s and 1960s aid flowed exclusively to Asia, hovering around 98 to 99 percent of total aid flows and reaching 100 percent in 1969.[1] Globalization of Japanese aid began under the Tanaka Kakuei cabinet in the early 1970s. Following the first oil crisis in 1973, Tanaka dispatched Deputy Prime Minister Miki Takeo, Minister of International Trade and Industry Nakasone Yasuhiro, and LDP politician Kosaka Zentaro to the Middle East and Africa; Tanaka himself journeyed to Brazil and Mexico.[2] Economic aid served as a nice "gift" during those visits. (Aid policy is often referred to in Japan as "gift diplomacy," or *omiyage gaiko*.)

Throughout that decade, Asia's share of aid decreased while the other Third World regions' portion increased noticeably. In 1972 Asia absorbed 98 percent of total Japanese ODA, while the Middle East received 0.8 percent, Africa 1 percent, and Latin America 0.6 percent. In 1981 Asia's allocation declined to 70 percent, while the Middle East's share increased to 8.4 percent, Africa's to 9.3 percent, and Latin America's to 7.8 percent.[3] (See table 5-1.)

Throughout the 1970s aid experts began to advocate the need for a broader focus for aid policy, especially as Japan entered the ranks of the economic giants. "The fact that Japan became an economic great power and the second largest contributor of aid tells us that it must look to the world, not just Asia," argued one Japanese economist.[4] This feeling carried through into the 1980s, most recently reflected in the report of the Ad Hoc Commission on Administrative Reform, created under Suzuki to devise programs and suggestions for streamlining government administrative structures and policies. The Commission, in a report submitted to Nakasone, proposed a broader, multidimensional international cooperation policy that included relations with advanced nations and socialist countries as well as the developing nations.[5] This view is a variant of the "aid great power" theme that achieved some popularity in the early 1980s, with its underlying assumption that Japan has an obligation to increase aid spending commensurate with its economic strength.

While Japanese concern for energy and raw material sources spurred the globalization of aid in the 1970s, the further expansion since the Ohira cabinet reflects greater interest in Third World political developments. But differences exist in the degree of Japan's interest in each of these Third World regions.

Latin America

The United States plays a major role in defining Japan's political focus on this region. The Suzuki cabinet responded to U.S. calls to support President Reagan's Caribbean Basin Plan. In 1980 the World Bank predicted negative economic growth and severe balance of payments problems for Jamaica, a nation with inconsequential trade relations with Japan. The United States was anxious to support Prime Minister Edward P. Seaga, who had ousted the socialist Michael Manley government in the October 1980 elections. Secretary of State Alexander Haig requested Foreign Minister Okita Saburo to

Table 5-1
Regional Distribution of Japan's Bilateral ODA
$ millions (percent)

	1972	1973	1974	1975	1976	1977	1978	1979	1980	1981
Asia	466.73 (97.7)	673.07 (88.0)	762.50 (86.0)	638.03 (75.0)	581.25 (77.2)	533.03 (59.3)	923.45 (60.3)	1,331.51 (69.3)	1,382.51 (70.5)	1,604.51 (71.0)
Northeast Asia	114.38 (23.9)	137.73 (18.0)	156.64 (17.8)	75.98 (8.9)	10.92 (1.5)	73.84 (8.2)	55.45 (3.6)	48.07 (2.5)	81.69 (4.2)	320.77 (14.2)
Southeast Asia	295.71 (61.9)	411.53 (53.8)	480.11 (54.5)	425.92 (50.1)	425.68 (56.5)	307.65 (34.2)	588.26 (38.4)	791.74 (41.4)	860.93 (43.4)	929.03 (41.1)
ASEAN	241.43 (50.5)	321.03 (42.0)	360.95 (41.0)	380.36 (44.7)	358.80 (47.7)	269.07 (29.9)	449.41 (29.4)	572.06 (29.8)	703.38 (35.9)	799.68 (35.4)
Southwest Asia	55.66 (11.6)	117.40 (15.3)	123.41 (14.0)	132.83 (15.6)	142.32 (18.9)	147.31 (16.4)	263.57 (17.2)	477.17 (24.8)	434.93 (22.2)	350.29 (15.5)
Other Asia	0.98 (0.2)	6.41 (0.8)	2.34 (0.3)	3.30 (0.4)	2.33 (0.3)	4.23 (0.5)	16.17 (1.1)	14.17 (0.7)	4.96 (0.3)	4.42 (0.2)
Middle East	3.83 (0.8)	10.59 (1.4)	22.25 (2.5)	90.41 (10.6)	58.98 (7.8)	219.99 (24.5)	347.78 (22.7)	203.45 (10.6)	203.61 (10.4)	190.07 (8.4)
Africa	5.01 (1.0)	18.49 (2.4)	36.23 (4.1)	58.82 (6.9)	45.93 (6.1)	56.25 (6.3)	105.49 (6.9)	186.72 (9.7)	222.91 (11.4)	210.53 (9.3)
Latin America	2.72 (0.6)	35.24 (4.6)	39.51 (4.5)	47.21 (5.6)	49.48 (6.6)	79.23 (8.8)	131.79 (8.6)	165.97 (8.6)	118.48 (6.0)	176.52 (7.8)
Pacific Islands	1.43 (0.3)	15.21 (2.0)	13.42 (1.5)	0.21 (*)	0.53 (0.1)	1.30 (0.2)	2.87 (0.2)	2.22 (0.1)	1.46 (0.1)	2.28 (0.1)

Source: Gaimusho Keizai Kyoryoku Kyoku Seisaku Ka, *Keizai Kyoryoku ni Kansuru Kihon Shiryo* (February 1983), p. 21.
*Negligible.

provide assistance to Seaga, and the Japanese responded in 1981 with their first loan to Jamaica of $10.1 million in commodity loans. The Nakasone cabinet responded with two additional loans of $25 million and $47 million in 1983.[6]

Japan has recently given special attention to Mexico, the Dominican Republic, Honduras, El Salvador, and Costa Rica in Central America. In South America official flows have recently focused on Peru, Brazil, Paraguay, Bolivia, and Colombia. (See table 5–2.) But under Suzuki, officials denied the political and strategic implications of aid to Central America and the Caribbean. "It is not security-linked strategic aid," a Foreign Ministry official insisted.[7] The government turned even more cautious after the killing of a Japanese business executive in Costa Rica during a kidnap attempt by Salvadoran guerrillas in 1982.[8]

Cuba, a nation with strained relations with the United States, poses a problem for the Foreign Ministry. Officials find it difficult to argue the denial of aid because of differences in political systems, since Tokyo does aid communist nations, and they hesitate to invoke international behavior as a criterion (despite the Vietnam case). Thus the Japanese provide a miniscule percentage of technical assistance to Havana and justify the lack of loans and grants on the grounds that "the extent of interdependence is low." One official suggested in an intraministerial meeting that the government should acknowledge the existence of exceptional cases like Cuba and Vietnam that transcend interdependence and humanitarian criteria.[9]

Table 5–2
Japanese Yen Loans to Latin America, 1984
billion yen

Country	Amount	Share (%)
Peru	50.3	16.3
Brazil	40.3	13.0
Paraguay	37.2	12.0
Mexico	30.0	9.7
Bolivia	26.7	8.6
Ecuador	20.3	6.6
Jamaica	18.3	5.9
Honduras	17.5	5.7
Colombia	33.0	10.7
Dominica	12.2	4.0
Nicaragua	7.5	2.4
Costa Rica	6.8	2.2
El Salvador	5.7	1.8
Chile	2.7	0.8
Total	308.5	

Source: Yoshitaka Yoshino, "Restoring Good Investments in Latin American Nations," *Look Japan*, March 10, 1985, p. 17.

In Latin America Japan's primary interest in the region remains economic despite the advent of political interest and selective uses of strategic aid. Strategic concerns appear grafted onto foreign economic policy at the behest of Washington. Trade statistics indicate a standard pattern of manufactured products flowing from Japan to Latin America (including machinery, transportation equipment, chemicals, and durable goods) and raw materials flowing to Japan. Trade patterns reveal a high concentration of Japan's economic relations in the major aid recipients, including Mexico, Brazil, and Panama for exports (which received over half of Japanese exports between 1980 and 1984) and Brazil, Mexico, and Venezuela for imports (accounting for two-thirds of total imports from the region during the same period).[10]

While supportive of American requests for immediate, short-term strategic aid for specific nations, Japan views economic development and stability as long-term objectives in the region. Thus the Japanese have focused increasingly on the debt crisis in the 1980s. Japan hopes to assist Brazil, Mexico, and Argentina in particular in repaying their accumulated debts, of which Japanese banks hold 15 percent of the total regional debt.[11] In the summer of 1985, the government decided to encourage the extension of new yen loans to nations which had deferred debt repayments. Unlike other DAC donors, Japan had refrained from extending yen credits to about 20 such nations in Africa and Latin America. Reports indicate that the government's reconsideration of that policy included the importance of the political situation in the region.[12]

The Japanese have turned high-level attention to the region in the 1980s, especially since the start of the Reagan administration. Prime Minister Suzuki attended the Cancun Summit in Mexico and stopped in Brazil and Peru enroute home. Foreign Minister Abe Shintaro represented the Nakasone cabinet's interest in the region by visiting Central and South America and the Caribbean in 1983 and 1985. The government dispatched a "project-finding" aid mission to Honduras, Colombia, Paraguay, and Peru in 1984, a delegation composed of officials from the Foreign Ministry, MITI, the EPA, the OECF, and JICA. And in July 1985, Abe informed Secretary of State George Shultz that Japan will increase aid to Honduras, Costa Rica, El Salvador, the Dominican Republic, and other Latin American states.[13]

Japan has traditionally viewed Latin America as an American preserve and was a latecomer to aid activities in the region. The private sector had taken the lead in building relations with nations in the region, especially in the 1970s. Private flows continue to predominate substantially over ODA, but in the 1980s, Japanese political interests followed the Reagan administration's spotlighting of the region, first by designating El Salvador a frontline state and then by urging international support for Contra rebels struggling against the Sandanista government of Nicaragua. In spring 1985, the Japanese government pledged anew to increase aid to Latin America and the Caribbean amid congressional debate in the United States over economic and military assistance to the Contras.[14]

Africa

Japan's links with Africa have been exceedingly thin historically. Hardly any contacts existed in the prewar period. A spark of interest flared in the 1950s, as these nations gained independence and joined the Afro-Asian movement, with the 1955 Bandung Conference as a high point. Japanese interest flagged, however, as African nations experienced domestic difficulties, creating an image in Japan of a region beset by civil strife and coups d'état. Japanese still retain the image of a dark continent, backward and unstable, where Japan has few stakes politically or economically. In the 1960s the Japanese became aware of Black African nationalism and activism in the international arena, but it was the oil shock in the early 1970s that heightened awareness of Africa's potential role as an important source of energy resources. In the early 1980s Japanese attention has been captured by the droughts and famines that afflict some of the poorest peoples in the world.

Japan traditionally considered Africa the preserve of the French. Tokyo has therefore given little attention to the continent in aid policy and provided minimal assistance to French-speaking West African states. The humanitarian coloring of Japanese aid has been especially strong, and that coloring deepened in the 1980s with the attention given to refugee assistance in the Sudan and famine relief efforts in Ethiopia.[15] In 1981 one-half of aid to Africa went to the Sub-Saharan region, with 60 percent in the form of grants.[16]

Trade relations developed slowly, and "whether an African country had natural resources or not was a decisive factor in Japanese trade with that country." Therefore, "Japan tended to trade with such countries regardless of their domestic political problems or of whether a great deal of international criticism was directed against them [that is, trade with South Africa]."[17] Economic aid, according to one study, thus followed Japan's economic interests by concentrating on major trade partners: Kenya, Madagascar, Niger, Sudan, Tanzania, Zaire, and Zambia. Four-fifths of Japanese aid to the region between 1960 and 1981 flowed to these seven countries.[18] However, in recent years, these countries only partially overlap Tokyo's major trade partners in the region (the top 10 consisting of South Africa, Nigeria, Liberia, Libya, Egypt, Algeria, Kenya, the Canary Islands, Zambia, and Ghana).[19] Most of these states do correspond to nations Japan now considers politically important on that continent.

Japan responded to Western concerns over Libya's attempt to destabilize the government of Sudan by pledging a $26 million loan in 1982. This ended a four-year hiatus in loans to Sudan.[20] Tokyo also views Tanzania as a leader in the dialogue between the nations of the North and South and considers Kenya and Zimbabwe as keys to regional security.[21] Japan also views Zambia, Nigeria, and the Ivory Coast as politically important Black African countries.[22] Nigeria, Kenya, Zambia, and Tanzania constitute four of the top five African recipients of yen loans (as of mid-1982).[23]

Japanese attention to African affairs remains overshadowed by interest in Asian and Middle Eastern events. Tokyo's attention to Africa is a recent, 1980s, phenomenon. The government is less equipped to follow regional developments, maintaining embassies in only 21 of the 51 African nations.[24] No prime minister has visited the region, and prior to 1980, only two foreign ministers have journeyed to African nations, each after an oil crisis: Kimura Toshio visited Ghana, Nigeria, Zaire, Tanzania, and Egypt in 1974, and Sonoda Sunao stopped in Nigeria, the Ivory Coast, Senegal, Tanzania, and Kenya in 1979.

Government attention to Africa heightened during the Suzuki cabinet for political reasons. The Foreign Ministry has dispatched its parliamentary vice minister (a Liberal Democratic Party politician and not a career bureaucrat) to five or six countries each year since 1981. In 1984, under Nakasone, Parliamentary Vice Minister Kitagawa Ishimatsu visited Zambia, Malawi, Madagascar, the Central African Republic, and Somalia; he declared that parts of Africa would fall under Soviet influence unless Western nations extend African nations a helping hand.[25] Foreign Minister Abe followed in November 1984 with visits to Zambia, Ethiopia, and Egypt.[26] The government now consistently expresses its intention to upgrade Japan's attention to regional developments in Africa.

The Middle East

Based on history, one would expect extremely thin relations between Japan and the Middle East, given the geographic distances involved and the large cultural gap between these societies. In many ways, however, Japan has paid greater attention to the Middle East at the official level than to any other Third World region historically, including Southeast Asia. Government-level interest in Southeast Asia emerged only in the 1930s, since Japan accepted that region as the colonial preserve of the British, French, and the Dutch, but official interest in the Middle East extends back to the previous century.

In the late nineteenth and early twentieth centuries, the Meiji government looked to the Middle East as a dual model. On the one hand the government studied such countries as Turkey and Egypt as models for terminating unequal treaties imposed on Japan by Western nations (that is, to abolish extraterritoriality and to restore tariff autonomy). On the other hand, as Japan began its imperialistic quest for empire, Egypt and North African territories (Tunisia, Algeria, and Morocco) served as reverse models that were useful in instructing Japan on how to administer its newly acquired imperial possessions, especially Taiwan and Korea.[27]

Japanese interest in the region abated once the unequal treaties were abolished and Japan's grip on its empire solidified. Official concern resurfaced in the 1960s, sparked first by the 1967 Arab-Israeli "Six-Day War" and the 1973 oil crisis. The main fear concerned Japanese oil supplies since inexpensive oil had served as the lubricant of the postwar industrial machine and "economic miracle." Prior to 1973 the government had found it unnecessary to deal directly with Arab governments to secure oil. The major oil companies served as go-betweens in oil transactions. The rise of the Organization of Petroleum Exporting Countries (OPEC) and the flexing of its political and economic muscles ended that arrangement. Henceforth, Japan would have to deal with Arab governments directly.

Tokyo scurried to establish direct and close relations with oil-producing countries immediately. In December 1973 the Tanaka Kakuei cabinet dispatched a special envoy to eight Middle Eastern nations. Liberal Democratic Party faction leader and soon-to-be prime minister Miki Takeo received a carte blanche authorization from the government to use economic assistance as a means to establish friendly relations. Former Foreign Minister Kosaka Zentaro, Speaker of the House of Representatives Maeo Shigesaburo, and MITI Minister Nakasone Yasuhiro followed Miki to the region. Japan's strategy aimed at an "energy-for-expertise trade off," as Japan offered $3 billion in aid to Arab states, including $1 billion each to Iran and Iraq.[28] The strategy succeeded, according to one view, because the Arabs curtailed oil cutbacks and placed Japan on a list of "friendly nations."[29]

That was just the beginning for Japanese activities in the region, for ever since the first oil shock, Japan has shown an increased willingness to contribute to regional peace and security. The Ohira cabinet significantly increased economic assistance to Egypt as a sign of support for President Anwar Sadat's peace initiative toward Israel (by journeying to Israel), and for the Jimmy Carter–Anwar Sadat–Menachem Begin Camp David Accords of 1978. Between 1977 and 1980 Egypt, already a consistent top 10 Japanese aid recipient, received $441.64 million. During that period Cairo was the fifth largest recipient of Japanese aid and certainly the largest non-Asian recipient.[30] By the mid-1980s Egypt enjoyed the highest rate of annual yen credit increases of any Japanese aid recipient, with over 40 percent of the funds devoted to projects on the Suez Canal.[31]

The Japanese also allowed the Palestine Liberation Organization to set up a representative office in Tokyo, and the Suzuki cabinet expected to host visits by both Sadat and his antagonist PLO leader Yassir Arafat in 1981. Only Arafat arrived, since Sadat was felled by assassins' bullets in Cairo.[32] Sadat's successor, Hosni Mubarak, thus became the first Egyptian head of state to visit Tokyo (in April 1983, during the Nakasone cabinet). Nakasone and Mubarak established a Joint Economic Committee to discuss economic and technical cooperation on a regular basis, and Nakasone pledged a 50 million yen credit.

Japan values Mubarak's Egypt as a leader in the nonaligned world and as a key to peace in the Middle East. Cairo controls the Suez Canal, exports 200,000 barrels of oil per day and functions as a moderate, stabilizing force in the region. Mubarak's meeting with Arafat in December 1983 pleased the Japanese, who take the position that peace is impossible without the inclusion of the Palestinians in any solution. Japan looks with favor on Mubarak's attempt to mitigate Egypt's estrangement from its Arab neighbors, which emerged under Sadat.

Despite the clear strategic overtones of Japan's relations with Egypt, the government had been hesitant to acknowledge the strategic relevance of its aid to domestic audiences. The Ohira cabinet placed Egypt outside the "countries bordering areas of conflict" formula, while the Suzuki government relied on interdependence and "areas which are important to the maintenance of peace and stability of the world." The government makes a point of distinguishing between Japan's economic assistance and the aid given by other nations: The United States, France, and the United Kingdom provide Egypt with military assistance; West Germany and Japan extend purely economic cooperation, according to one source.[33] The Nakasone government is less skittish about the real purpose of aid to Egypt.

The Suzuki cabinet gave prominence to the Persian Gulf states, while aid to Iran and Iraq tailed off after the American hostage crisis and the eruption of the Iran-Iraq conflict. It began to focus on North Yemen, troubled by the marxist government of South Yemen, and Oman. Oman, a nation with a population of about one-tenth Tokyo's, lies astride the strategic Strait of Hormuz and controls the flow of 70 percent of Japan's oil supply (and 65 percent of West European and 30 percent of American supplies). Attention also focused on Saudi Arabia, a pivotal state from Washington's perspective. In 1981 the Suzuki cabinet extended $100 million to Saudi Arabia through the OECF for a petrochemical project.[34]

The Gulf states also represent the core of Japan's economic relations with the Middle East. Major trade partners include Saudi Arabia, the United Arab Emirates (UAE), Iraq, Iran, Kuwait, Qatar, and Oman. In 1980 the gulf states absorbed 80 percent of Japan's exports to the Middle East, and one analyst asserts that by 1979, the importance of the region as an export market for Japan exceeded that of ASEAN.[35] Gulf states provided a staggering 97 percent of all imports from the region, mostly petroleum.[36] OPEC nations in 1980 provided 80 percent of Japan's oil, with Saudi Arabia, the UAE, and Iran serving as the primary suppliers.[37]

Japan's political interest in the region is largely a 1980s phenomenon. To some extent Japan responded to American and European involvement. For example Japan responded to U.S. requests in 1983 to participate in rebuilding war-torn Lebanon in cooperation with other Western nations. Tokyo agreed to assist in repairing telecommunications systems in Beirut and had considered shouldering part of the cost of maintaining a multilateral peacekeeping force following an Israeli withdrawal from Lebanon.[38] In other areas American and Japanese interests coincide, including an agreement on the importance of Saudi Arabia, and on other issues, Japan and the United States are said to differ, especially on policy toward Iran.[39]

The Nakasone cabinet has taken another look at relations with Iran following the conclusion of the American hostage crisis and the outbreak of the Iran-Iraq conflict in 1980. The war threatened to further destabilize the region, erupting between the Soviet invasion of Afghanistan and American withdrawal from Lebanon after the killing of 241 Marines. While Japan felt powerless to effect any changes in Beirut, the Iran-Iraq conflict seemed different. There, Japan felt situated in a unique position: While Iranian and Iraqi relations with the United States and West Europe were estranged or hostile, Japan maintained good relations with both combatants.

Japan took special care in maintaining cordial relations with Iran in the wake of the hostage crisis. For example, Mitsui and its partners sought to withdraw from its involvement in a large-scale petrochemical project, Bandar Khomeini. The Japanese government forced Mitsui to maintain its involvement, with the government providing funds to what it now designated a national project. The government's intentions were political: A withdrawal would have damaged relations with Iran and other Middle Eastern countries, opened the way for Soviet influence, and isolated Iran from all Western nations.[40]

Since the conflict contributed to maintaining that region in turmoil, and since Western nations had little leverage or influence over Iran or Iraq, the Japanese began efforts to mediate the dispute. Since 1983 Tokyo has invited high-level officials of both countries, separately, to discuss the situation. Japanese envoys have also journeyed to the region, including Foreign Minister Abe, who visted Iran and Iraq's regional allies (pro-Iran Syria and pro-Iraq Saudi Arabia and Jordan).[41]

The Japanese have proposed a cease-fire and a mutual agreement on the part of the combatants to exempt ships in Gulf waters from military attack. Efforts to date have proven unsuccessful and the Japanese remain guarded about their chances for success. But Japanese involvement in mediation efforts is a significant development in Middle East policy and overall foreign policy. Japan has declared its readiness to support stabilization and peace efforts in the region by contributing economic and technical assistance.

Of all the Third World regions outside of Asia, Japan has paid closest attention to developments in the Middle East as an international trouble spot that affects the interests of all Western nations as well as Japan. Actual participation in the politics of the region, however, has been restrained, even under an "activist" Nakasone cabinet. One problem is that the "rest of the Third World" cannot compete with Japan's attention to Asia.

Regionalism

"Japanese aid should retain its regional focus," insists a Finance Ministry official. "Africa should be left primarily for France and the Commonwealth countries to Britain. Japan's contribution should not be zero, but it should remain in Asia."[42] Figures show that 70 percent of British aid flows to Commonwealth members, 90 percent of French aid to French-speaking areas, especially in Africa, and 40 percent of U.S. aid to Egypt and Israel.[43] The Japanese feel this is natural and are comfortable with this configuration.

This deep-seated Japanese conviction is based on both pragmatic and emotional criteria. Given limited financial resources available for ODA, Japan should concentrate on neighbors with whom Japanese share a common heritage, history, culture, economic philosophies, and political values. Never mind that much of this must be qualified with respect to Japan-Asian relations, but the Japanese do retain a strong emotional identification with the Asian region. China, Korea, and the ASEAN states also constitute major sources of raw materials (including oil, liquefied natural gas, timber, natural rubber, copper, bauxite) and vibrant current and potential markets for manufactured goods (including vehicles, textiles, chemicals, iron and steel products, and technology). Government officials express a resolve to halt the slide of Asia's share of total aid flows at the current 70 percent level, while Africa, Latin America, and the Middle East are to receive roughly 10 percent each.

The government does not highlight the fact that the concepts "countries bordering areas of conflict," "areas which are important to the maintenance of peace and stability of the world," and even "comprehensive national security" were all designed initially to apply primarily to Asian nations. Note, for instance, that Pakistan and Thailand do fit the "bordering conflict" criteria (with Afghanistan and Kampuchea as neighbors, respectively), but Turkey stands out. Thailand's case is most clear-cut for the Japanese: "Thailand is a country on which Japan places top priority in considering its assistance to ASEAN because of its importance in the area and also as a country bordering areas of conflict."[44] Turkey is far from Afghanistan and is not threatened by immediate threats from conflicts on its border. Japan assumes Turkey to be a Western, NATO responsibility and its own role as peripheral. One official ranks Thailand at the top of the priority list, with Turkey as the least important and Pakistan's status somewhere in between.[45]

The director of the Foreign Ministry's Economic Cooperation Bureau notes that the inclusion of Egypt and Turkey among the top 10 recipients in 1981 represents a broader dimension in aid policy but stresses that Asia will continue to be the central focus for aid extended under the "areas which are important to the maintenance of peace and stability of the world" concept, with ASEAN as top priority.[46] Japan's bilateral aid is clearly intended primarily for Asia.[47] As for comprehensive security, ASEAN serves as the model for the use of economic assistance to preserve national security. Aid to ASEAN members promotes national economic growth and prosperity in the region; this contributes to political stability in Asia; and stability in Asia benefits the West as well as Japan's comprehensive security.[48]

Despite the increased outflow of aid to other Third World regions, aid figures still reveal Asia's dominant position in Japanese policy. In 1983 all of the top 10 recipients were Asians. (See table 5-3.) Of the top 10 aid recipients between 1978 and 1981, nine were Asian nations, with Egypt the only exception. Of the nine, five were Southeast Asian, four of which were ASEAN members (with Burma the fifth Southeast Asian nation).[49] (See table 5-4.) Indonesia, traditionally the leading recipient, topped the list with $1.1 billion. Thailand ranked second between 1978 and 1981 with $687 million.

The Philippines received $460 million. Japan considers the Philippines increasingly important because of serious economic difficulties and political instability confronting the government of Ferdinand Marcos, especially after the assassination of Benigno Aquino. Tokyo consistently ranked Manila in the top five during the 1980s and steadily increased aid in the past two years (1983 and 1984). The Nakasone government pledged $271 million in 1984 (up from $147 million allocated in 1983) and $150 million in quickly disbursable commodity aid in 1985.[50]

Tokyo granted Malaysia $253 million, and Kuala Lumpur consistently ranked eighth or ninth on the top 10 list during the Suzuki and Nakasone cabinets despite a relatively high per capita income level. Tokyo, always conscious of Malaysia's strategic location astride the Strait of Malacca, also considers Malaysia a key to the settlement of the Kampuchean problem and to regional stability. The Nakasone cabinet in particular supports Prime Minister Datuk Seri Mahathir Mohamad's active diplomacy. Tokyo shares Malaysia's (and Indonesia's) softer, more conciliatory inclination toward relations with Vietnam as a means of countering Hanoi's strong dependence on the Soviet Union. Japan, however, does not share Malaysia's (and

Table 5-3
Top 10 Aid Recipients, 1983
($ millions)

Country	Amount	Share (%)
China	350.15	22.4
Thailand	248.12	15.8
Indonesia	235.46	15.0
Philippines	147.02	9.4
India	129.54	8.3
Burma	113.39	7.2
Bangladesh	104.20	6.7
Malaysia	92.30	5.9
Sri Lanka	73.08	4.7
Pakistan	72.77	4.6

Source: *Japan's Official Development Assistance 1984 Annual Report*, p. 8.

Table 5-4
Top 10 Japanese Aid Recipients, 1978-1981
($ millions)

Country	Amount	Share (%)
Indonesia	1,104.32	14.4
Thailand	687.63	9.0
Bangladesh	686.07	8.9
Burma	559.90	7.3
South Korea	492.16	6.4
Philippines	460.08	6.0
Pakistan	445.37	5.8
Egypt	445.12	5.8
Malaysia	252.97	3.3
Sri Lanka	173.34	2.3

Source: Ministry of Foreign Affairs, *Keizai Kyoryoku ni Kansuru Kihon Shiryo*, February 1983, p. 27.

Indonesia's) fear of the People's Republic of China, rather than Moscow, as the real long-term threat to Asian security. Japan would rather serve as a bridge between these regional forces.

Finally Japan is committed in particular to the Mahathir administration because of the prime minister's enthusiastic promotion of a "Look East" policy. Mahathir has ostensibly rejected Western models of economic development in favor of "Eastern" models, namely the Japanese (and to some extent, South Korea's) development experience. The Japanese, somewhat embarrassed by this national policy, thus developed a vested interest in the success of "Look East." A failure of Mahathir's program would reflect poorly on Japan.

A fifth ASEAN member, Singapore, receives mostly technical assistance because of its status as a high-income newly industrializing country.

Singapore devotes Japanese technical cooperation to human resources development. From Japan's point of view, Singapore also guards the Malacca Strait and is deeply involved in the politics of the Kampuchean issue. The Lee Kuan Yew government has been a major supporter of and catalyst for the coalition government (comprised of the Khmer Rouge, the Khmer People's National Liberation Front and the forces of Prince Nordom Sihanouk) that currently challenges the Vietnamese-backed government of Heng Samrin. In addition the Japanese feel an added responsibility to assist Singapore in some way because President Lee promotes his own version of a Look East policy, which he dubbed "Learn from Japan."

ASEAN receives one-half of its external assistance from Japan. Tokyo's share of Indonesian aid in 1981 was 37 percent, 68 percent for Thailand, 64 percent for the Philippines, 55 percent for Malaysia, and 58 percent for Singapore.[51] In terms of Japan's total outflow of ODA, ASEAN's share has consistently declined since the 1970s; Japan sent 51 percent of its aid to ASEAN members in 1972 and 36 percent in 1980 and 1981.[52] However, the absolute amount has soared. MFA officials indicate an intention to maintain ASEAN's share each year at approximately one-third of total ODA in the future.

ASEAN's formation in 1967 occasioned little Japanese official comment, especially since Tokyo was absorbed in its own regional efforts, including the creation of the Asian Development Bank and the Ministerial Conference for the Economic Development of Southeast Asia. Riots greeted Prime Minister Tanaka's 1973 ASEAN tour, in Indonesia and Thailand, and these incidents served as a catalyst for increased official attention to Southeast Asia. In addition the 1975 fall of Saigon and U.S. troop withdrawal from Southeast Asia and the rejuvenation of ASEAN at the 1976 Bali Summit highlighted the new group's potential importance in a fluid regional environment.[53]

All prime ministers since Tanaka Kakuei have paid close attention to Southeast Asia and especially ASEAN. Miki Takeo (1974–1976) devised an "Asian Marshall Plan," which disappeared with the Miki cabinet. Fukuda Takeo (1976–1978) unveiled the "Fukuda Doctrine" in Manila in August 1977. The Fukuda statement consisted of three major pledges: Japan will remain a peaceful nation, promote "heart-to-heart" relations with ASEAN nations, and deal with ASEAN as an equal partner while seeking a relationship of mutual understanding with the Indochinese states (Vietnam, Laos, and Cambodia). The centerpiece of Fukuda's ASEAN policy was a $1 billion pledge to assist ASEAN regional projects. Fukuda's declaration echoed past cabinets' thinking on Japan–Southeast Asian relations and previewed themes developed by successive governments. The $1 billion pledge remains unfulfilled, largely due to problems on the ASEAN side in determining and initiating the five regional projects, but it represented the debut of Japan's new aid diplomacy. For the pledge to ASEAN coincided with Fukuda's international commitment at the Bonn Summit to double Japan's ODA.

The ASEAN approaches of Fukuda's successors may not have been as spectacular, but they have been equally forceful. During a visit to Beijing, Ohira made clear to his Chinese hosts that ASEAN remains top priority in Japanese aid policy.[54] Suzuki Zenko chose to visit the ASEAN nations as his first official sojourn abroad, thereby breaking the tradition established by his predecessors of paying respects to Washington before all others.

Suzuki concluded his tour in Thailand, the country his cabinet regarded as top priority in ASEAN.[55] In his final address of the trip, his "doctrine," Suzuki outlined four basic areas that Japan would emphasize: the development of rural and agricultural sectors; the development of new energy sources; the development of human resources (technical assistance); and support for small and medium-size industries. As one MFA aid official later explained, "What he had in mind was the development of Northeast Thailand, whose [sic] development is of utmost importance from both peace and stability and humanitarian points of view."[56] This approach, with strong emphasis on basic human needs, has become the core of Japanese aid policy in other Third World regions as well.[57] Japan has "ASEAN-ized," or perhaps "Thailand-ized," its aid policy.

The Suzuki cabinet established the 7:1:1:1 ratio for Asia and the other Third World regions. The government intended to continue flows to ASEAN totaling one-third of total disbursements, or a little less than one-half Asia's share. This constituted a further reason for Suzuki's hesitation on South Korea's aid demand. Six billion dollars would have taken the lion's share of Asia's allocation over the proposed five years and wreaked havoc on Japan's preference for gradual incremental increases in annual aid pledges and disbursements. Nakasone endorsed the $4 billion compromise and followed Suzuki's breaking of the visit-the-U.S.-first mold by visiting Seoul prior to Washington. Nakasone did not shift Suzuki's ASEAN priority in favor of South Korea, however, and he assured ASEAN leaders of his fidelity to the Ohira-Suzuki line in his 1983 keynote speech in Kuala Lumpur: "There will be no change in Japan's basic policy of regarding the ASEAN countries as the highest priority area for our assistance efforts."[58]

Although Nakasone extended around $1 billion in aid pledges to ASEAN nations during his May 1983 trip, he refrained from striking new policy innovations. He eschewed yet another "doctrine" and emphasized the need for Japan to consolidate past cabinets' promises and programs. Aside from scientific and technical cooperation, personnel exchanges and technology transfers, Nakasone also placed emphasis on plant renovation and revival of old projects, rather than finding new ones. This does not indicate a lack of interest in ASEAN, for Nakasone's discussions with ASEAN heads of state focused extensively on the political, diplomatic, and strategic situation in the region and other parts of the world. Nakasone, to the contrary, has shown increased interest in political and strategic dimensions of Japan's relations with East, Southeast, and South Asian nations.

Nakasone has not sacrificed regionalism in favor of globalism. On the contrary he appears to have deepened the emphasis on Asia. On his ASEAN tour he spoke of "solidarity," "feelings of kinship between Japan and the ASEAN people," and of "the spiritual and cultural heritage common to this East Asian region where Japan and the ASEAN countries are located."[59] He has also linked Japan and ASEAN to a "common destiny": "Without prosperity for ASEAN, there can be no prosperity for Japan."[60] A major goal of his ASEAN trip was the establishment of close, personal relations with heads of state, a comraderie that would allow regular, informal telephone calls between colleagues. Japan's relations with ASEAN blossomed into Tokyo's closest relationship with any of the Third World nations.

China

The Nakasone cabinet's strategic aid pattern today seems to emphasize reinforcement of Ohira and Suzuki initiatives in Asia while holding the line on new commitments outside the region. Within this framework China has developed into ASEAN's closest rival for Japanese aid in terms of amounts and special treatment. ASEAN views the growth of intimate Sino-Japanese ties uneasily. ASEAN governments sense that Japan considers China the real priority because of economic, political, historical, and emotional ties to the mainland. Their concern is understandable since the most outstanding development in Japanese aid policy in the 1980s is the sudden rise of China as Japan's principal bilateral aid recipient.

During the Maoist era China scoffed at foreign aid. Maoism stressed self-reliance and caution toward foreign influence and economic penetration. The Chinese accepted loan aid only from socialist nations ($1.5 billion) and only in the 1950s.[61] The Chinese were dissatisfied with the aid even from socialist nations, especially from the Soviet Union because of stringent terms and conditions. China viewed all foreign aid suspiciously, and not until after 1976 (after the fall of the "Gang of Four") did Beijing seriously consider economic assistance from abroad.

The catalyst and framework for aid emerged with Deng Xiaoping and the "Four Modernizations Policy," intended to propel China into an economic superpower by the next century. This ambitious goal required a loosening of Mao's strict self-reliance tenets in an effort to attract foreign capital and technology. For multilateral assistance, China joined the World Bank and sought membership in the Asian Development Bank. For bilateral aid the Chinese government turned to Japan.

Japan and China normalized diplomatic relations in September 1972, in the wake of the Sino-American rapprochement. In 1978 the two nations signed a Treaty of Peace and Friendship, following long and tough negotiations on the inclusion or exclusion of an antihegemony clause aimed at the Soviet Union. The clause remained, with Japan insisting that it does not apply to any third power. Tokyo and Beijing also concluded a Long-Term Trade Agreement, calling for an expansion of trade to $40 billion by 1990.[62]

Deng Xiaoping raised the issue of economic assistance during his 1978 visit to Tokyo, and in 1979, China presented Japan with a request for $5.5 billion for eight construction projects. Vice Premier Gu Mu pointedly singled out Japan as the first nation to which China had submitted a loan request. He also promised to procure equipment and machinery in Japan with the loan funds.[63]

Prime Minister Ohira, one of the architects of the 1972 normalization, became a sympathetic supporter of Deng's "Four Modernizations." His policy sought to do "anything possible to encourage stability and progress toward an open society in China, which is seen as the best way to insure Japan's national interests."[64] But Ohira did not accept the $5.5 billion request for aid. He encountered stiff criticism at home and abroad. Pro-Taiwan LDP members protested the special attention given to Beijing. Europe and the United States grew increasingly concerned with Japanese beachheads on the China market; Washington especially protested the tied nature of Japanese loans to China. The Soviet Union interpreted the Peace and Friendship Treaty as a Japanese decision to "lean to one side" in the Sino-Soviet dispute and viewed burgeoning economic links between Beijing and Tokyo with some alarm. ASEAN grew uneasy with Japan's support for a Chinese economy that was competitive rather than complementary with ASEAN economies; and ASEAN realized that $5.5 billion for China could mean less aid for Southeast Asia.[65]

The Ohira cabinet sought to placate its domestic and foreign critics. It refused China's request for $5.5 billion. The Chinese modified the figure to $2 billion, but Ohira accepted $1.5 billion for six of the eight proposed projects (plus $61 million for a Chinese hospital, designated as a symbol of bilateral friendship). The funds were to be untied, meeting a U.S. objection to tied loans for China, and distributed over a three- to six-year period.[66] But even the reduced $1.5 billion figure caused anxieties in Tokyo because it exceeded the Fukuda cabinet's 1977 pledge to ASEAN of $1 billion for its regional projects. As a result, when the aid agreement was announced in Beijing, no mention was made of the total amount of Japan's pledge. Only the figure for the first year's installment saw the light of day.[67] And further, the Japanese devised a formula whereby the Chinese annual loan total during the initial years would not exceed the amount granted to the number one bilateral aid recipient (at the time, Indonesia).[68] In other words China would not shoot to the top of the top 10 list in such a spectacular fashion, at least overnight. China did not enter the top 10 until 1982 primarily because of unilateral Chinese plant and contract cancellations or postponements in 1980–1981.[69]

Ohira's principal device for allaying the fears and criticism of foreign nations was the three principles or guidelines for aid to China announced during his 1979 visit to Beijing. First, Ohira pledged to cooperate with the West in assisting Chinese modernization efforts, a pledge aimed at Western Europe and the United States. Second, Ohira pledged to give priority to ASEAN in foreign and economic policy. Third, the prime minister promised to refrain from extending military assistance to China, an effort to disassociate Japan from involvement in the Sino-Soviet split.[70]

For all of the government's attention to ASEAN in the 1980s, one cannot help but wonder if Beijing receives top-priority consideration. The sensitive textbook controversy in 1982 (of concern to China because of a proposed softening of the depiction in high school textbooks of the Rape of Nanking) failed to disrupt the commemoration of the 10th anniversary of the normalization of relations. Premier Zhao Ziyang visited Tokyo and Prime Minister Suzuki journeyed to Beijing, where Deng Xiaoping announced that the textbook controversy had been settled to China's satisfaction. During negotiations with the South Koreans on the $6 billion aid demand, Tokyo insisted that multiyear aid commitments were difficult because of Japan's annual appropriation procedure for the aid budget. Yet Japan informally agreed to fulfill multiyear commitments to China during negotiations for China's first loans in 1979.[71]

Even the serious setbacks in bilateral economic relations in 1980–1981, including unilateral project cancellations, failed to prevent China's meteoric rise to Japan's list of top 10 aid recipients.[72] In 1982 China debuted at the top, surpassing Indonesia, with $389 million (to Jakarta's $295 million). In 1983 China received $350 million, overshadowing Thailand's notable rise above Indonesia to gain the second spot.[73] The rise of China as the number one bilateral aid recipient has been notable, if not spectacular, given Japan's penchant for slow, incremental commitments of aid amounts to individual recipients.

What has made China special is Japan's recognition of a new opportunity to influence and affect the course of political and economic developments within China in a way that was impossible during the Mao Zedong years. Through aid policy, the Nakasone cabinet made explicit what Ohira and Suzuki preferred to keep implicit—that Deng Xiaoping's liberal policies offer an excellent opportunity to encourage and promote a more open, stable, and friendly China; a China that is politically stable and economically prosperous will contribute to regional peace and stability; and such developments can only work to the mutual benefit of both Japan and China.

For the Japanese, foreign aid has become part of the cement that solidifies Sino-Japanese political relations. It reflects a growing convergence in recent years of Chinese and Japanese views on such issues as the Soviet invasion of Afghanistan, the Soviet military buildup along the Sino-Soviet border, Soviet naval presence and buildup in the Asia Pacific region, the Vietnamese incursion into Kampuchea, and the situation on the Korean peninsula. Nakasone's talks with Chinese leaders during his March 1984 visit to Beijing focused precisely on these political-strategic issues, as Nakasone pledged an additional $2 billion in aid to China. Nakasone's focus heightens—or confirms—the strategic and political equation behind Japan's aid to China. Japan will continue to provide strong support for Deng Xiaoping and his policy direction.

Despite the appearance of a Japanese preference for China over ASEAN in aid policy, Japan remains highly sensitive to ASEAN concerns. In April 1983 Chinese Vice Premier Yao Yilin requested another aid package, this time for $6 billion (a figure perhaps influenced by South Korea's $6 billion demand to the Suzuki cabinet).[74] Nakasone whittled the amount down to a still substantial $2 billion, for seven development projects.[75] In the process the prime minister strongly reaffirmed his commitment to Ohira's three principles on Chinese aid, including the priority to ASEAN. And while China did reach the top position as the largest aid recipient in 1982 and 1983, in both years Thailand, Indonesia, the Philippines, and Malaysia together received almost twice China's share.

Japan has no intention of sacrificing good relations with ASEAN in favor of a closer relationship with China. Japan regards political stability and economic development in both sectors crucial for regional stability and Japanese security. Tokyo prefers a closer relationship between China and ASEAN. Nakasone attempted a reconciliation between China and Indonesia during his 1983 ASEAN trip. Among the ASEAN states, Malaysia and Indonesia view China as the long-term threat to the region, and Singapore and Indonesia lack diplomatic relations with Beijing (with Singapore vowing to be the last to do so). China requested that Nakasone approach Indonesian President Suharto about the possibility of restoring the official relations severed in 1965. Suharto, however, refused to consider a normalization.[76]

Pakistan

Political overtones also dominated Nakasone's interaction with another of Ohira's strategic aid priorities, Pakistan, a "country bordering conflict." Heads of state Nakasone and President Mohammed Zia Ul-Haq exchanged official visits in 1983 and 1984 for the first time in a quarter century. In addition to the usual economic aid pledges ($170 million for 1984–1985), Nakasone visited a refugee camp at Peshawar during his May 1984 visit and pledged $14.9 million to assist Pakistan in caring for an estimated three million refugees from Afghanistan, a doubling of the $7 million pledge made to Zia in 1983.[77]

While Ohira and Suzuki seemed satisfied with supplying economic and refugee assistance, Nakasone attached a quid pro quo for his aid: Information from Islamabad on Soviet activities in the Middle East. Zia reportedly impressed Nakasone with a detailed briefing on Soviet moves in Afghanistan during his Tokyo visit in 1983. The two leaders established a Japan-Pakistan Joint Committee: "It was originally conceived that the joint commission would hold discussions centering on economic affairs, but security problems were added to the agenda at Nakasone's request."[78]

When Nakasone returned from Pakistan, he stated that Japan "should apply economic power more effectively in its diplomacy" and "cannot refuse to use economic cooperation for the purpose of mitigating tensions." He continued, "The way Japan can contribute to the world is economic cooperation and technical cooperation. Foreign policy is finding the road toward their application."[79] Again, Nakasone has taken steps to make explicit what Ohira and Suzuki sought to keep implicit in the use of aid for strategic purposes, but Nakasone remains within the framework established by his predecessors. This is illustrated by his cabinet's reaction to the Vietnam aid freeze, increases in aid to Laos and reaction to American requests to emphasize non-Asian aid recipients for strategic reasons.

Indochina

Nakasone's attention to Asia extends to socialist Asia other than China, as well as to ASEAN nations and the Indian subcontinent. His cabinet has not closed the door to better relations with North Korea despite the $4 billion commitment to South Korea. Also, as Nakasone's second cabinet began to function in 1983, officials pondered invitations to top political figures in and cultural exchanges with Mongolia. Further, the cabinet decided to extend increased economic assistance to Laos and has renewed communication links to Vietnam.

The Ohira cabinet froze all economic assistance to Vietnam after the invasion of Kampuchea, except for a trickle of humanitarian technical assistance to a hospital. Nakasone reaffirmed Japan's commitment to support ASEAN's call for a complete withdrawal of Vietnamese troops from Kampuchea, but he also indicated his willingness to assist in the reconstruction of Indochina once hostilities ceased.[80]

Officially, the Japanese supported the Reagan administration's condition for the resumption of normal relations, but they differ with the U.S.

"policy of isolation and pressure," as explained by a State Department official in 1981:

> The course of action most likely to result in the removal of Vietnamese troops from Kampuchea is to make the occupation as costly as possible for Hanoi. We will continue a process of diplomatic isolation and economic deprivation until Hanoi is prepared to follow the will of the world community . . . and agree to troop withdrawal.[81]

Ohira and Suzuki were overtaken by the mood and emotion of the times following the Kampuchean invasion and outwardly maintained strong and full support for America's hardline policy. Nakasone has returned to a pre-Ohira-Suzuki formula for dealing with Indochina, a formula articulated by Fukuda Takeo. The 1977 Fukuda Doctrine envisaged an active Japanese role in the region that emphasized ASEAN but not at the cost of alienating Vietnam. The Japanese had perceived the emergence of a new regional cold war after the fall of Saigon. It viewed the polarization of the region into two hostile blocs, the five ASEAN versus the three Indochinese states. Tokyo had expected to play a bridge-building role in promoting a reduction of tension between the two forces. That premise collapsed as the socialist "bloc" disintegrated with hostilities between Hanoi and the Pol Pot regime in Kampuchea, resulting in the Vietnamese ouster of the Khmer Rouge. But in the 1980s the situation stagnated, with the Vietnamese holding firm in Kampuchea and the ASEAN nations retaining the support of the majority of nations in the United Nations for the coalition government in exile.

While Ohira and Suzuki maintained a moratorium on high-level talks between Japan and Vietnam, the Nakasone cabinet has reopened lines of diplomatic communication. In March 1983 Tokyo invited Vietnamese Deputy Foreign Minister Ha Van Lau to Tokyo for talks, the first such talks since February 1978, and dispatched the director of the Foreign Ministry's Asia Bureau, Hashimoto Hiroshi, to Vietnam in December.[82] In May 1984 Foreign Minister Abe met again with Ha at the annual meeting of ESCAP (the UN's Economic and Social Commission for Asia and the Pacific) in Tokyo. Abe proposed a meeting between himself and his counterpart, Nguyen Co Thach, at the September UN General Assembly meeting. In October Thach and Abe met in Tokyo, ending a four-year hiatus on high-level talks and a six-year hiatus on talks between foreign ministers.[83]

The Japanese continue to reiterate their commitment to the aid freeze as long as Vietnamese troops remain in Kampuchea,[84] but the hard commitment has a soft core. After the imposition of the freeze, Japan rescheduled the repayment of Vietnam's debts, continued to import products from Vietnam and increased official representation in Hanoi.[85] In the spring of 1985, 26 Japanese banks agreed to reschedule $160 million in trade credits incurred during 1977 and 1978.[86] The Liberal Democratic Party engaged in an intensive debate over the freeze option, with Ohira's position prevailing. However, the party's official position makes clear that Japan remains willing to resume aid at the first opportune moment.[87]

The Japanese basically prefer a more conciliatory approach to Vietnam, including a preference for positive rather than negative uses of economic assistance in modifying Vietnamese behavior and in attempting to wean Hanoi from its dependence on the Soviet Union. This preference became apparent under Nakasone in policy initiatives toward the settlement of the Kampuchean problem and toward relations with Laos.

In June 1984 Foreign Minister Abe proposed a three-step settlement for Kampuchea: A Vietnamese troop withdrawal, a general election in Kampuchea, and the resumption of Japanese economic and technical assistance to Vietnam.[88] Abe stated that Japan is prepared to provide Indochina with "as much aid as possible." Foreign Ministry spokespersons supplied an intriguing detail: Vietnam might receive equal consideration with ASEAN in aid policy, a pronouncement certain to heighten concern in ASEAN nations. Abe also announced that Japan is willing to finance any international peacekeeping force dispatched to oversee any withdrawal of Vietnamese troops from Kampuchea.[89]

In July 1985 Abe suggested a four-point proposal: the withdrawal of Vietnamese forces from Kampuchea and self-determination for the Kampuchean people; promotion of dialogue between Vietnam, the Vietnamese-backed Heng Samrin government and the three-party coalition government opposed to Heng; reaffirmation of support for the coalition government; and a pledge of economic aid to Kampuchean refugees in Thailand for educational and vocational training. The aid would be part of the Japanese government's emphasis on human resources development in Asia.[90]

The Japanese effort to break the stalemate in Kampuchea has become a foremost example of a more active and involved Japanese foreign policy that consciously and willingly uses ODA as a diplomatic tool. It points to a Japanese conviction that their influence can be used most effectively in Asia, and that economic rather than military strength provides political leverage. Relations with Vietnam also reveal a distaste for the use of aid as a negative sanction to punish a nation's behavior. They basically prefer the use of aid as a positive sanction to reward or induce favorable attitudes and actions.

The Japanese preference for the conciliatory approach is also reflected in the Nakasone cabinet's initiative toward Laos. In 1983 the government approved $7 million for the construction of a pharmaceutical center despite doubts among some ASEAN members, especially Indonesia. (Thailand and Singapore endorsed the aid during Nakasone's visit, according to officials who accompanied Nakasone.) The Japanese justify the decision on the grounds that Laos is not involved in Kampuchea, is the Indochinese country most independent of the Soviet Union, seeks restoration of normal relations with the West, opposed Vietnam's Indochinese federation plan (in February 1983), serves as a buffer between Thailand and Vietnam and is a less developed nation that requires humanitarian assistance.[91]

The increase in aid to Laos reflected an extension of Japan's basic policy since 1975. Tokyo continued aid to Laos throughout the tumultuous events following the fall of Saigon. The government had been considering increases since 1980.[92] The LDP aid policy statement notes that Japan joins West Germany, Holland, Australia, Sweden, and others in providing aid to Laos, which contributes to peace and stability in the region.[93] While some observers interpret Japanese aid as an attempt to drive a wedge between Laos and Vietnam and thereby increase tension in the region,[94] the government emphasizes the humanitarian rationale to justify the medical aid. Given the humanitarian nature of the aid and the socialist government, left-wing parties in Japan have not protested this aid increase.

Initial ASEAN concerns centered on a possible crack in the anti-Vietnam economic embargo. Part of the problem was Japanese timing, coming at a time when a new Australian government under Bill Hayden began advocating resumption of his country's aid to Hanoi. ASEAN feared a Japanese effort to signal to Vietnam their willingness to resume aid before a withdrawal of troops from Kampuchea, and that medical supplies produced by the Laotian center would find their way to Kampuchea in the hands of Vietnamese troops. Japan reassured ASEAN that the aid freeze will remain intact and that Japan would monitor the project.[95] ASEAN approved a continuation, according to one MFA official, but not an increase in Laotian aid.[96]

The Foreign Ministry actually viewed ASEAN's complaints as hypocritical. Indonesia once had a similar plan in mind, notes one official, and Malaysia had established a fund for similar purposes. The major issue, in MFA officials' view, is who takes such initiatives. ASEAN just does not want Japan to take any kind of leadership role in the region. Another example occurred in spring 1983, when Japan attempted to convene a conference on the Kampuchean problem between ASEAN, Vietnam, Laos, and Japan. ASEAN opposed the proposal, telling the Japanese that Kampuchea is a matter between ASEAN and Indochina. Indonesia shortly thereafter proposed a similar idea.[97]

In Asia Nakasone has filled in and embellished the aid policy of his two immediate predecessors. He has remained within the Ohira-Suzuki framework. Radical departures from past policies are not visible, as Ohira and Suzuki's preferences on ASEAN, Indochina, and China have become Nakasone's policies. Strategic aid has progressed steadily in the Asian region.

Washington

The United States attempted to broaden the geographic scope and pace of Japanese aid policy in 1983 but ran into a wall of reluctance even from the staunchly pro-American Nakasone cabinet. At an OECD conference in March, the U.S. representatives reportedly presented Japanese delegates with a list of 20 countries for aid consideration, selected for their strategic importance.[98] The list is said to have included the following: South Korea, the Philippines, Thailand, Pakistan, and Indonesia in Asia; Egypt, Lebanon, and Israel in the Middle East; Honduras, El Salvador, Jamaica, and Costa Rica in Latin America; Sudan, Morocco, Tunisia, Somalia, and Kenya in Africa; and Greece, Portugal, and Spain in the Mediterranean, NATO's southern flank.[99]

At a bilateral aid meeting in June, the U.S. side suggested that Japan limit its aid to Asia and increase it to regions of the free world threatened by aggressive Soviet behavior. The Japanese side took pains to stress that Asia remains top priority in Japan's aid policy, based on comprehensive security interests and on the specific economic development situation in the region as it affects Japan. Support for other regions must be premised on these considerations.[100]

Washington and Tokyo agreed in 1982 to embark on joint aid projects in third countries. Japan was to focus on funding infrastructure and the United States on technical assistance.[101] The two nations have cooperated before informally in population control projects in Indonesia, an education project in Tonga and a refugee project on Bataan in the Philippines. The trilateral approach was formally inaugurated with an agricultural research project at Khon Kaen University in Northeast Thailand.

Again, these cases continue to indicate Japan's primary interest in Asian aid recipients. A Foreign Ministry explanation of why Japan supports joint projects with the United States focuses entirely on Asia and the South Pacific, referring specifically to Indonesia, the Philippines, Thailand, and Tonga and to consultations between Japanese embassies and U.S. Agency for International Development missions in Nepal, Pakistan, and Sri Lanka.[102]

When the possibility of joint projects emerged in a concrete way in 1982, aid-policymakers on both sides of the Pacific held high hopes for U.S.-Japan aid cooperation. Each maintained that the other side viewed aid as a potential cooperative field that would offset the tension and friction that plagued economic and defense arenas. Both sides lowered their expectations, however, as difficulties emerged in the coordination of respective policies and approaches. The Thai project commenced slowly, and the initial momentum may have been stymied. Differing U.S. and Japanese budget cycles hindered smooth coordination; aid philosophies differed; and problems often emerged with the third country government. By mid-1983, the MFA's attitude reflected a feeling of "If it happens, fine. If not, we'll push ahead on our own."[103]

If Japan had hopes that the economic aid field could be immune from political friction, those hopes may have been shattered in 1984 when the

United States used multilateral aid as a political weapon against Japan. Washington temporarily blocked Japan's bid to become the second largest contributor to the World Bank until Tokyo instituted a series of measures to open and deregulate its domestic financial market.

Japan will continue to stress Asia in aid policy for the foreseeable future. Any forays beyond the region will be highly selective, especially if aid has strategic objectives, and any sustained effort outside Asia may well depend on continual "monitoring" by other nations if the initial momentum is to be maintained. This limit on strategic aid expansion reflects domestic politics, but popular opinion in this case also reinforces the leadership's own reluctance to leave Asia. As one Japanese delegate to a 1982 U.S.-Japan aid meeting observed, when the U.S. delegates raised the issue of assistance for Liberia, Chad, Costa Rica, Sudan, and other nations, "They are very far away from Japan."[104]

Notes

1. See charts in Alan Rix, *Japan's Economic Aid* (New York: St. Martin's Press, 1980), p. 34.

2. Shigekazu Matsumoto, "Progress and Policy Formulation of Japan's External Assistance," paper delivered at "The U.S. Congress and the Japanese Diet: Conference on Comparative Studies in Foreign Policy," Honolulu, February 9–12, 1983, p. 7.

3. Japan, Ministry of Foreign Affairs, Economic Cooperation Bureau, *Keizai Kyoryoku ni Kansuru Kihon Shiryo*, February 1983, p. 21.

4. Toshio Shishido, *Tonan Ajia Enjo o Kangaeru* (Tokyo: Toyo Keizai Shimposha, 1973), p. 29.

5. Rinji Gyosei Chosakai Jimukyoku, *Rincho: Kihon Teigen; Rinji Gyosei Chosakai Dai 3-ji Toshin* (Tokyo: Gyosei Kanri Kenkyu Sentaa, 1982), p. 41.

6. *Asahi Shimbun*, March 9, 1982; *Nihon Keizai Shimbun*, July 15, 1983; *Asahi Shimbun*, May 12, 1983; and *Asian Wall Street Journal*, March 23, 1981; and William L. Brooks and Robert M. Orr, Jr., "Japan's Foreign Economic Assistance," *Asian Survey* 25(March 1985):333.

7. *Asahi Shimbun*, June 20, 1983.

8. See *Japan Times*, November 11, 1982.

9. Japan, Ministry of Foreign Affairs, "Anzen Hosho Seisaku Kikaku Iinkai Dai 3 Raundo, Dai 3 Kaigo Yoroku," April 28, 1982, pp. 7–8.

10. See Michael Chinworth, "Japan and Latin America: Economic and Political Relations," *JEI Report* (April 5, 1985). Panama's position as the top Japanese export market is idiosyncratic. Panama acquires ships from Japan under the flags of convenience rubric. See Akio Hosono, "Japan and Latin America," in Robert S. Ozaki and Walter Arnold, eds., *Japan's Foreign Relations: A Global Search for Economic Security* (Boulder, Colo.: Westview Press, 1985), p. 201.

11. Chinworth, "Japan and Latin America," p. 2.

12. *Yomiuri Shimbun*, June 3, 1985.

13. See Yoshitaka Koshino, "Restoring Good Investments in Latin American Nations," *Look Japan*, March 10, 1985, pp. 16–17, and *Yomiuri Shimbun*, July 13, 1985.

14. *Japan Times Weekly*, April 6, 1985.

15. *Asahi Shimbun*, October 8, 1984.

16. William L. Brooks and Robert M. Orr, Jr., "Japan's Foreign Economic Assistance," unpublished manuscript, p. 20.

17. Hideo Oda and Kazuyoshi Aoki, "Japan and Africa: Beyond the Fragile Partnership," in Ozaki and Arnold, eds., *Japan's Foreign Relations*, p. 153.

18. John Ravenhill, "Japanese Aid to Africa," *New African* (May 1983):40–41. See also, Oda and Aoki, ibid.

19. David Morris, "Japanese Trade with Africa," *New African* (May 1983):41–44.

20. *Japan Economic Journal* (March 23, 1982).

21. Brooks and Orr, "Economic Assistance," unpublished manuscript, p. 20.

22. Koichiro Matsuura, "'Keizai Kyoryoku Taikoku Nihon' e no Michi," *Keizai to Gaiko* (March 1982):19.

23. Masaaki Tamagami, "Economic Cooperation with Sub-Saharan Countries: Credits Targeted at Creation of Infrastructure," *Look Japan*, September 10, 1982, pp. 16–17.

24. *Asahi Shimbun*, October 6, 1984.

25. *Japan Times Weekly*, June 30, 1984.

26. *Japan Times Weekly*, December 8, 1984.

27. San-eki Nakaoka, "Studies on Egypt's Legal System Conducted by Japanese Bureaucrats in the Early Meiji Era," in *Arab-Japanese Relations* (Tokyo: Japan National Committee for the Study of Arab-Japanese Relations, 1980), pp. 135–40.

28. Michael Yoshitsu, *Caught in the Middle East: Japan's Diplomacy in Transition* (Lexington, Mass.: Lexington Books, 1984), p. 7; and Terutomo Ozawa, *Multinationalism Japanese Style* (Princeton, N.J.: Princeton University Press, 1979), p. 144.

29. Ozawa, *Multinationalism*, p. 145.

30. Japan, Ministry of Foreign Affairs, Economic Cooperation Bureau, "Japanese Economic Cooperation," February 1, 1982, p. 8.

31. Keiichi Matsumoto, "Japan-Egypt Economic Cooperation: Focus on Infrastructure for a Strategic Power," *Look Japan*, June 10, 1984, p. 15.

32. See Yoshitsu, *Caught in the Middle East*, pp. 23–38.

33. Matsumoto, "Japan-Egypt," p. 15.

34. See Yoshitsu, *Caught in the Middle East*, p. 85.

35. William R. Campbell, "Japan and the Middle East," in Ozaki and Arnold, *Japan's Foreign Relations*, pp. 142–3.

36. San-eki Nakaoka, "Recent Economic Relations Between Japan and the Arab World," in Japan National Committee for the Study of Arab-Japanese Relations, *Arab-Japan Relations: Mishima Symposium* (Tokyo: Japan National Committee for the Study of Arab-Japanese Relations, 1982), pp. 62–63.

37. See Campbell, "Japan and the Middle East."

38. *Mainichi Daily News*, July 14, 1983.

39. See Yoshitsu's study, *Caught in the Middle East*.

40. Ibid., pp. 82–103.

41. *Yomiuri Shimbun,* July 7, 1985.

42. Interview with a government official, July 11, 1983.

43. Toshio Aoki, "Japan's Official Development Assistance to Asian Countries," *Journal of Japanese Trade and Industry* (May-June 1983): 59.

44. Koichiro Matsuura, "Japan's Economic Cooperation with ASEAN; Assistance Will Never Fail To Grow," *Mainichi Daily News,* September 30, 1981.

45. Matsuura, "Taikoku," p. 33.

46. Kenichi Yanagi, "Konnichi no Sekai to Nihon no Enjo," *Kokusai Kyoryoku* (March 1983): p. 9.

47. Matsuura, "Taikoku," pp. 32–33.

48. Koichiro Matsuura, "Sogo Anzen Hosho Seisaku toshite no Keizai Kyoryoku," address delivered at the Sogo Anzen Chosakai, Dai Yon-kai Kenkyukai, April 4, 1981, p. 9.

49. Japan, Ministry of Foreign Affairs, *Kihon Shiryo,* p. 21.

50. Brooks and Orr, "Economic Assistance," p. 331.

51. Japan, Ministry of International Trade and Industry, Tsusho Seisaku Kyoku, "Nichi-Bei ASEAN Keizai Kankei no Kongo," *Boeki to Sangyo,* June 1983, p. 32.

52. Japan, Ministry of Foreign Affairs, *Kihon Shiryo,* p. 21.

53. For recent Japan-ASEAN relations, see Alan Rix, "ASEAN and Japan: More Than Economics," in Alison Broinowski, ed., *Understanding ASEAN* (London and Basingstoke: The MacMillan Press, 1982), pp. 169–95.

54. Shinkichi Eto, "Recent Developments in Sino-Japanese Relations," *Asian Survey* (July 1980): p. 740.

55. Matsuura, "ASEAN" in *Mainichi Daily News,* September 30, 1981.

56. Ibid.

57. Brooks and Orr, "Economic Assistance," p. 13.

58. *Asahi Shimbun,* May 9, 1983; and *Mainichi Daily News,* May 10, 1983.

59. *Japan Times,* May 10, 1983; and *Mainichi Daily News,* May 10, 1983.

60. *Asian Wall Street Journal,* March 2, 1983.

61. Chae Jin-Lee, *China and Japan: New Economic Diplomacy* (Stanford, Calif.: Hoover Institution Press, 1984), p. 113.

62. Walter Arnold, "Japan and China," in Ozaki and Arnold, *Japan's Foreign Relations,* p. 103.

63. Lee, *China and Japan,* p. 116.

64. Eto, "Sino-Japanese," p. 740; and Minoru Aoki, "Bijon Naki Nihon no Keizai Enjo no Jittai," *Ajia* (May 1982): p. 77.

65. Lee, *China and Japan,* pp. 113–18.

66. Eto, "Sino-Japanese," pp. 740–1.

67. Ibid., p. 741.

68. Related in Lee, *China and Japan,* p. 122.

69. On these delays and cancellations, see Arnold, "Japan and China," pp. 102–18.

70. Eto, "Sino-Japanese," p. 740.

71. Lee, *China and Japan,* p. 122.

72. Aoki, "Bijon," p. 77.

73. *JEI Report* (September 1984); and *Japan Times Weekly,* March 16, 1985.

74. *Asahi Shimbun*, April 2, 1983; *Daily Yomiuri*, April 5, 1983; and *Japan Economic Journal* (January 25, 1983).

75. Shumitsu Miyazawa, "Japan-China Economic Cooperation: New Yen Credits for Infrastructure Development," *Look Japan*, May 10, 1984, pp. 16–17.

76. See *Daily Yomiuri*, May 2, 1983; and *Asian Wall Street Journal*, March 2, 1983.

77. *Japan Times Weekly*, May 19, 1984 and April 7, 1984.

78. *Daily Yomiuri*, July 24, 1983.

79. *Asahi Shimbun*, May 4, 1984.

80. *Mainichi Daily News*, May 10, 1983.

81. U.S. Senate Committee on Foreign Relations, Subcommittee on East Asia and Pacific Affairs, *First Session on U.S. Policy Objectives in Southeast Asia and the Factors Which Shape These Objectives; U.S. Policy in Southeast Asia; July 15, 21, and 22, 1981* (Washington, D.C.: U.S. Government Printing Office, 1981), p. 6.

82. *Nihon Keizai Shimbun*, March 10, 1983; and *Asahi Shimbun*, January 9, 1984.

83. *Japan Times Weekly*, October 20, 1984.

84. Interview with an MFA official, June 13, 1983.

85. Nayan Chanda, quoted in Robert W. Barnett, *Beyond War: Japan's Concept of Comprehensive National Security* (Washington and New York: Pergamon Brassey's International Defense Publishers, 1984), pp. 117–18.

86. *Far Eastern Economic Review* (May 30, 1985): 12.

87. Liberal Democratic Party, Policy Affairs Research Council, Special Committee on Overseas Economic Cooperation, *Waga To no Keizai Kyoryoku Seisaku ni Tsuite* (Tokyo: Jiyu Minshuto Seimu Chosakai, 1982), pp. 136–7.

88. *Japan Times Weekly*, October 20, 1984.

89. Charles Smith, "Japanese Middle Man," *Far Eastern Economic Review* (September 29, 1984): 42–43.

90. *Yomiuri Shimbun*, July 22, 1985.

91. Interviews with government officials, June 13, 1983 and July 12, 1983; and *Yomiuri Shimbun*, June 29, 1983; *Mainichi Shimbun*, June 29, 1983 and July 26, 1983; *Mainichi Daily News*, June 6, 1983; and *Asahi Shimbun*, June 29, 1983.

92. Interviews at the Foreign Ministry, June 13, 1983 and July 12, 1983.

93. Liberal Democratic Party, *Waga To*, p. 136–7.

94. *Mainichi Daily News*, June 6, 1983; and Yuji Suzuki, "Gunkaku to Fukyo no Naka no Keizai Kyoryoku," *Sekai*, July 1983, p. 63.

95. Interview with MFA official, July 12, 1983, and interviews at ASEAN embassies in Tokyo, spring and summer 1983.

96. *Asahi Shimbun*, June 29, 1983.

97. Interview with government officials; and Isamu Ogiso, "Kisha no Me: ASEAN ni Furimawasareru na," *Mainichi Shimbun*, July 21, 1983.

98. *Mainichi Shimbun*, June 19, 1983.

99. Compiled from interviews with Japanese and American aid officials, and *Mainichi Shimbun*, May 5, May 25 and June 19, 1983; *Mainichi Daily News*, June 19, 1983; and *Japan Times*, May 1, 1983.

100. *Mainichi Shimbun,* June 19, 1983; and *Mainichi Daily News,* June 19, 1983.

101. Brooks and Orr, "Japan's Foreign Economic Assistance," pp. 338–9.

102. "Nichi-Bei Kyodo Purojekuto no Tenkai," Undated MFA document (the dates August 1 and 15, 1982 are written by hand in the margins).

103. Interviews with officials.

104. Related by an American aid official present at the meeting.

6
The "Legacy" of Strategic Aid

> First ponder, then dare.
> —Helmuth Von Moltke

J apan's economic assistance policy developed throughout the postwar
period as a component of foreign economic policy. Beginning with
reparation payments to Southeast Asian nations in the 1950s and
1960s, Japan's recovery from wartime devastation and the subsequent
"economic miracle" received a boost from the extension of aid to develop
overseas markets and secure needed raw materials. In the 1970s Tokyo
utilized foreign aid to stabilize the flow of energy resources in the wake of
the first oil shock, and this entailed a globalization of aid allocation to
Africa, Latin America, and the Middle East. Throughout these years the
Japanese retained the primacy of economic and resources rationales rather
than a strategic justification for aid. Japan consciously separated politics
from economics.

From 1977 through the mid-1980s, successive Japanese cabinets accentuated and accelerated aid policy. The Fukuda Takeo cabinet announced
the first pledge to double ODA in 1977 and took the first step by commit-
ting $1 billion dollars to ASEAN nations. Prime Minister Ohira Masayoshi
inaugurated strategic assistance by promoting the conceptualization of
comprehensive national security and initiating aid to "countries bordering
areas of conflict." Suzuki Zenko balked at the extension of aid to South
Korea explicitly for strategic uses, but the prime minister favored strategic
uses of aid in general as a substitute for the military buildup and efforts
demanded by the United States. Strategic aid developed under Suzuki as aid
to "areas which are important to the maintenance of peace and stability of
the world," which served as one rationale for the globalization of political
aid to Third World areas beyond the Asia Pacific region. Nakasone Yasuhiro has made increasingly explicit what Ohira and Suzuki sought to keep
implicit to domestic audiences. Strategic aid is now an acknowledged
foundation and underpinning of economic assistance policy.

By the mid-1980s ODA policy has lost its one-dimensional economic
character. No other country has embarked on an aid-expansion policy
as enthusiastically as Japan; to the contrary, many donor nations are

hard-pressed to justify money for foreigners amid economic austerity at home. No other nation has raised foreign aid to the status of a central pillar of foreign policy; to the contrary most nations continue to regard aid as a limited or peripheral support of foreign policy. No other country has professed such strong dependence on ODA for its national security; to the contrary, economic aid is considered secondary to military policy in effectiveness as a weapon in the national security arsenal.

Why did the Japanese elevate aid policy to central diplomatic pillar, and why cast it in a strategic light? Economic assistance policy, including strategic aid, emerged from the political closet in the 1980s as part of a broader Japanese effort to define an active rather than passive international role rooted primarily in national economic rather than national military strength. Foreign aid is one of the building blocks of that new international role.

What does Japan specifically hope to accomplish through the use of national economic strength, and how does aid policy fit into the equation? The Japanese seek five interrelated objectives, and aid contributes to the attainment of all five goals.

1. Economic Well-being. The Japanese seek to maintain economic growth and their affluent lifestyle. Economic aid contributes toward that goal by helping to secure raw material and energy resources in the Third World, and to maintain Third World markets during a time of trade friction and rising protectionist moods in the First World. By assisting developing nations to cope with internal economic problems, the Japanese hope to preserve the international economic system that proved so crucial to their economic miracle.

2. National Prestige. The Japanese are translating economic strength and accomplishments into a heightened international status. Economic achievements contribute to a resurgence of self-confidence and pride scarred by the World War II experience. Aid policy has a demonstration effect: The ability to grant ODA symbolizes Japan's attainment of membership in the "rich men's club" while displaying an attitude of concern, largess, and cooperation toward the nations of the South. Japan, the second largest economy in the free world, attained the status of second largest contributor to the World Bank and the second largest contributor (in terms of amount) of bilateral ODA in 1984. For Japan these were symbolic but significant milestones in the effort to bolster national prestige.

3. Domestic Support. Postwar Japanese governments enjoyed a national consensus on the need to concentrate all energy on economic reconstruction and development. Domestic political controversies centered primarily on security-related issues, but few challenged the goals and direction of national economic policies under the Liberal Democratic Party. The LDP reaped the political benefits of the economic miracle at the polls, remaining entrenched in power for three decades of uninterrupted rule. As Japan attained the postwar economic goals of reconstruction, growth, and prosperity and catching up with the West, the LDP is attracted to any policy that can engender another consensus. Economic aid currently enjoys popular support among a broad spectrum of interests, including the mass media, bureaucrats, business interests, labor unions, public opinion, the LDP itself, and all opposition parties. Therefore, from the government's perspective, why not capitalize on the growing popular support for a more active foreign policy by designating as a main support one component that enjoys a favorable national consensus—the use of foreign aid for humanitarian and interdependence uses. The ruling party in other words reaps political benefits from the promotion of economic aid policy.

4. Peace Diplomacy. While Japanese public opinion increasingly recognizes Japan's need for an active foreign policy, the Constitution and the enduring spirit of Japanese pacifism continue to place legal, political, and psychological constraints on the role Japan can play in world affairs. The Japanese people do not favor a substantial military buildup, an expansion of Japan's regional security role, or a foreign policy based on military strength. Nor would Japan's Asian neighbors, ever suspicious of Tokyo's defense policy, agree to such a definition of diplomatic activism. Both parties prefer a nonthreatening peace diplomacy rooted in national economic strength. Economic aid thus becomes the prime candidate for emphasis almost by default. For many Japanese economic aid policy offers a means of escaping from the island country mentality and foreign policy passivity in favor of "doing something" without the risks of dependence on military power. The use of aid for strategic purposes serves as a substitute or supplement for an unwanted military buildup.

5. National security. The Japanese define national security broadly, to include nonmilitary as well as military threats and countermeasures. However, Japan, a nation that lives by a "trade or die" ethic, places greater weight on the nonmilitary side of the scale. Nonmilitary threats can bring the nation to its knees as effectively as a military invasion, including such eventualities as the stoppage of energy resources and foodstuffs or the closure of overseas markets to Japanese exports. Therefore Japan's best defense is a good offense that stresses preventive diplomacy based on nonmilitary diplomatic methods and countermeasures, including economic aid policy. According to this reasoning, the selective use of aid can economically and politically stabilize countries and regions of strategic importance to Japan. A continued judicious use of ODA can nurture and maintain friendly relations that would prevent policies hostile to Japan. And since Western allies consider these Third World nations critical to international security, a militarily weak Japan can contribute to Western alliance interests by utilizing its economic and financial strength. Through strategic aid, Japan can concurrently preserve its national interests as a good, loyal Western ally.

These five overlapping, interrelated objectives define Japan's attempt to translate national economic strength into an activist, involved foreign policy geared for the world of the 1980s and beyond. Successive cabinets have designated economic assistance, and its strategic uses, an integral component of the new diplomatic look. But the fact that aid fits comfortably into all five objectives signifies its chameleon-like nature and places strategic aid in perspective. This flexibility explains much about its ability to survive in a domestic political environment that remains wary of security issues, but it also reveals much about strategic aid's ambiguities and limitations. Ambiguities and limitations are not fatal for strategic aid, however, because it is woven into the fabric of Japan's international aspirations for the future.

Concepts and Ambiguities

Strategic aid has survived in a skeptical domestic environment *because* of conceptual ambiguity. Comprehensive national security, countries bordering areas of conflict, areas which are important to the maintenance of peace and stability of the world, interdependence, humanitarianism—these concepts are strategic aid's relatives, but none can claim parentage.

"Countries bordering conflict" emerged under Prime Minister Ohira and applies to only three countries: Thailand, Pakistan, and Turkey. "Areas which are important to the maintenance of peace and stability of the world" debuted in the Reagan-Suzuki joint communiqué to cover all other strategically related aid recipients. The use of aid under comprehensive national security, promoted by Ohira and adopted by Suzuki as national policy, includes policies involved with energy, foodstuffs, and other components. The interdependence theme recognizes Japan's reliance on the international economic system and the need for maintaining friendly relations with economically and politically important nations. Interdependence and humanitarian considerations constitute the two overriding official justifications for economic cooperation policy today.

One can easily perceive the utility of these concepts in explaining or justifying aid policy. To the United States and the Western alliance, the government can say that Japan is deeply involved in supporting countries besieged by turmoil on their borders (countries bordering conflict) or regions of importance not only to Japan but also the West (areas which are important to the maintenance of world peace and stability). At the same time, the government can argue that strategic aid is the most it is able to do because of constitutional and political restrictions on military defense policy. Comprehensive security recognizes the limits of military power and the ascendancy of nonmilitary threats to the nation and the need for nonmilitary countermeasures like economic aid. To the nations of the South, Japan can affirm its understanding of the common destiny shared with the developing nations. As a non-Western nation that attained prosperity without sacrificing its traditional culture, Japan can claim to fulfill obligations to the South based on interdependence and humanitarian criteria.

Domestically the government can reverse the order and emphasis. To its own people cabinets can argue that humanitarian aid demonstrates Japanese concern for and generosity toward the less fortunate of the world. At the same time, the nation, dependent on critical resources and markets in the developing world to maintain its current standard of living, needs to develop friendly relations in the Third World. Aid is a major and often only substantial official link with many developing nations. Occasionally, specific nations, especially in Asia, require extra assistance to maintain political and economic stability. Japan must, therefore, extend strategically oriented emergency aid in its own interest. But this will not be military assistance; it will be aid based on interdependence and humanitarian considerations from a nation able to afford these expenditures. This aid activism will gain the respect of foreign nations eager to see Japan contribute more to international affairs. Aid, then, allows Japan an opportunity to rely on a peace diplomacy based on economic rather than military capabilities.

In practice, "countries bordering areas of conflict" and "areas which are important to the maintenance of peace and stability of the world" are not distinct and different components of a broader comprehensive security policy. They are the same, seeking identical goals of stability and friendly relations with nations deemed important to Japan and the West, and through the same aid tools—yen loans, grants, commodity aid, and technical assistance. In practice, little difference exists between Turkey, Pakistan, Korea, Egypt, and the other priority nations in terms of the intended impact of aid.

Moreover, much of Japan's aid is "mixed." Aid officials separate interdependence, comprehensive security, and humanitarian considerations, but economic assistance in practice is a complex policy arena. Aid's impact is difficult to assess. The case of South Korea is officially cited as an example of interdependence, but both interdependence and security implications and rationales are deep and intertwined. Jamaica and Tanzania, for example, are instances of minimal interdependence and increasingly significant political importance. Brazil and Mexico do not lack political importance for Japan, but interdependence seems the greater criterion for aid.

Economic aid given for purely interdependence reasons may have military implications. Project loans for highway construction may benefit peasants transporting produce to markets, but they can also increase the mobility of government troops and military equipment against insurgents. Dam projects can be used to flood guerrilla-held territory as well as provide electric power to a region.[1]

Even humanitarian aid is not immune from strategic coloring. The humanitarian character of aid to Bangladesh and many Sub-Saharan African countries is clear, but aid for Afghan refugees in Pakistan and Kampuchean refugees in Thailand contains obvious strategic and political implications. Aid to Laos, officially justified as humanitarian aid, carries strong political overtones, and the trickle of technical assistance to the hospital outside Ho Chi Minh City keeps open a communication link to Vietnam. Economic assistance to ASEAN countries reveals a combination of humanitarian, interdependence, and strategic considerations.

Conceptual ambiguity should not obscure the fact that Japanese aid policy has traveled a long road in a short period of time toward the open, explicit inclusion of political and strategic considerations. This has not proved fatal to strategic aid policy; it has survived quite nicely. To the contrary, the government may be underestimating potential support among the people for increased aid for political reasons. The uproar over the Korean aid issue may have been a special case—poorly presented by the Koreans, poorly handled by the Japanese and lasting for a long year and a half period. The issue rapidly faded from the headlines after the settlement, after the government's expected assurances about the nonmilitary intent of the aid and after opposition parties had their day in the Diet. The general public is hardly aware of the aid to Jamaica, and its rejection of assistance to oil-rich Oman or to Chinese neighbors is highly unlikely. Aid to ASEAN would undoubtedly continue to receive strong support, and even aid to the Indochinese states may receive strong backing if presented as part of a peace diplomacy aimed at reducing regional tensions. Ambiguous relationales may have provided the lead time necessary for the gradual acceptance of strategic uses of aid among the populace. A people that can accept the legitimacy of the SDF, the need for the U.S.-Japan Security Treaty and a nonmilitary emphasis on comprehensive security seems ready to accept in principal strategic aid given openly in certain specific cases.

In this sense the problem of strategic aid rests not with the people alone. Their feelings about defense and security issues are understandable given the wartime experience and the postwar cultural, social, economic, and political milieu. Part of the problem rests in the lack of self-confidence on the part of the national leadership. Political leadership is an essential requirement for strategic aid policy's survival and evolution. The domestic aid policymaking apparatus is dispersed, compartmentalized, and prone to infighting involving numerous ministries and agencies. Popular support for aid is not translated into active aid lobbying, especially for strategic uses of aid.

Immediate crises receive top priority in the government, especially the trade friction with the United States and other trade partners. If the leadership's attention and commitment falters, strategic aid policy will falter.

On the one hand recent cabinets may be viewed to date as having assessed aid policy in a pragmatic realistic manner. From this perspective the survival and progress of strategic aid merely represents a combination of the leadership's reading of the public mood, recognition of legal, political, and emotional constraints, personal preferences for a concentration on Asia, adherence to stringent budgetary limits and recognition of the need to respond to foreign pressure. The government in other words has successfully and skillfully shepharded strategic aid through treacherous terrain based on perceived needs and capabilities. On the other hand, while focusing on immediate policy needs in a pragmatic manner, the government has difficulty responding to central questions that will determine the course of strategic aid policy in the future.

Problems

First of all, how, exactly, does economic assistance contribute to national security? The simple answer is: by promoting economic, social and political stability in recipient nations. This will, in turn, create a stable and peaceful regional and international environment; and this will redound to Japan's benefit politically and economically. However, aid does not produce results overnight. Unlike military assistance, which can beef up a nation's defense capabilities quickly, development aid will not produce "instant stability" or "instant development." Development assistance is a long-term proposition, but Japan's long-term development and political aid strategy is difficult to determine.

Futhermore, is aid enough, and will there be enough aid? If the Marshall Plan is considered a prototype of a successful venture in aid diplomacy, two critical elements stand out (besides the shared cultural heritage and stage of economic development of the European recipients): the massive flow of resources from the donor to the recipients, and the donor's willingness to resort to noneconomic, military methods to achieve limited and clearly defined objectives.[2]

Japan's aid policy cannot meet these standards even in Asia. The United States provided Western Europe over $40 billion between 1942 and 1952 (of which $33 billion was in grant form) and $43 billion more during the Eisenhower years (1952–1960).[3] Japan's record pales by comparison: about $1 billion a year to its priority area, ASEAN; fairly tough conditions and terms for bilateral ODA; and undefined political objectives. Tokyo could not meet even its modest commitment to double ODA in five years, and with the conclusion in 1986 of the aid-doubling plan, early indications reveal the government's hesitation in making another specific large increase pledge and in considering the annual aid budget a special case. Japan has a long way to go if it desires to be an "aid superpower."

America's determination to support Europe politically, economically, and militarily buttressed its willingness to underwrite the region's economic recovery. The United States did not rely solely on economic tools to achieve strategic objectives. The Marshall Plan succeeded within a framework of a military alliance, with substantial transfer of military equipment, aid, and personnel. The United States had been prepared to intervene militarily in the defense of Europe.

This framework and option does not exist for Japan even in the ASEAN area: "It is unlikely that Japan will ever resort to noneconomic means to rescue a developing Southeast Asian nation that has fallen into internal social unrest."[4] Political, legal, and emotional restrictions prohibit consideration of overseas military-type operations. Most important, Japanese will to intervene is lacking. Besides, the strongest opposition to an interventionist Japanese role in the Asian region comes from the Asian nations themselves. Perhaps Nakasone erred in linking Japan and ASEAN to a "common destiny."

Japan confronts problems when considering intermediate options as well. Diet resolutions prohibit the sale or transfer of military technology or military-related aid; nor can aid flow to nations involved in conflict if that aid would exacerbate tensions. Dual-use technology and equipment is a gray area. Political sensitivity currently places restrictions on this type of aid, but one could expect exploration of this option, especially in view of the U.S.-Japan agreement on military technology transfer and the periodic "testing" of Japanese resolve by recipient nations. Commodity aid remains the one aid form that allows recipient governments to convert funds for defense purposes. But the Japanese monitor and restrict its allocation and use. Japan would still need a flexible, quickly disbursable funding mechanism to circumvent a time-consuming budget process in emergency situations.

While Japan is aware of the need for a long-term view of ODA and large commitments of funds, and understands the need for supplementary diplomatic tools, aid analysts raise a nagging question that the Japanese have yet to address: Is economic aid really effective in achieving economic development and, consequently, political and social stability? Packenham flatly asserts:

> There appears to be no clear correlation between aid and economic development, to say nothing of aid and political development. Some of these countries which received substantial aid have realized no significant economic development, while some of the most impressive cases of economic growth and development occurred without the benefit of foreign assistance.[5]

The Reagan administration would concur, arguing that foreign aid actually retards development by increasing the role of the state in the development process while hindering the development and functioning of free market mechanisms and forces.

Knorr goes a step further by asserting that political instability and not stability, can result from foreign aid: "In fact, the immediate effects of sustained economic development are so disruptive of political, social, and cultural life that political instability is a likely consequence."[6] He explains that

> all foreign aid more or less affects the recipient society concerned, the capabilities of its government and economy directly, and its political and social life indirectly. All economic change generated by aid will advantage some people and disadvantage others. All economic progress, to the extent that it is engendered by external aid, is intrinsically disruptive to the established ways of economic and social life.[7]

Knorr also takes a dim view of the long-term prospects of aid-giving on the behavior of recipient nations: "Moreover, there is no historical support whatsoever for the expectation that the economic growth of poor countries produces internationally pacific conduct."[8]

These assertions strike at the heart of both short-term and long-term objectives and assumptions of Japan's strategic aid policy. The leadership has not faced these possibilities squarely, exhibiting instead a spirit of optimism and accentuating positive outcomes. The policymakers' search for domestic and foreign approval for aid policy does not allow them to dwell on the dire consequences, but a failure to explore such contingencies may result in the creation of overly high, unrealistic expectations. The 1981–1985 aid-doubling pledge is a good example of confidence and optimism leading to an international commitment that the government failed to fulfill. The long-run danger of ignoring negative consequences of politicized aid is disillusionment and the loss of that domestic consensus on aid that the government tries so hard to maintain and nurture. Aid's possible negative consequences is an aspect that must be addressed in any future study of Japanese strategic assistance.

The "Legacy" of Strategic Aid

What impact is strategic aid likely to have on future Japanese foreign policy? It may be premature to discuss the legacy of a policy so young and ill-defined, but at this stage in its development, four effects may be foreseen:

1. Strategic aid makes security consciousness respectable. Aid makes it possible both to acknowledge or advocate the need for increased security preparedness and to deflect charges of harboring militaristic or hawkish views. Aid presents an alternative to the sole reliance on a military buildup to

enhance national security. It softens the "defense=militarization" link that remains strongly embedded in the popular mind. Strategic aid can be considered an intermediate step between "economic animalism" and "militarism," and this is one of the appeals of comprehensive national security. The unlinking of the security-militarism image and the elevation of nonmilitary alternatives may have been one of Ohira's most important legacies, according to one view:

> What Prime Minister Ohira did achieve, and this may well be seen in later years as one of the more important of his political legacies, whether intentional or not, was to gain more widespread acceptance of a broader interpretation of national security in the consensus politics of Japan compared to the past. ... Above all, the debate about comprehensive security emphasized that, if the military component in Japanese security policy were to be brought into line with the level of resources and the degree of priority accorded to it in other liberal democratic societies, the ending of the defence anomaly in Japan need not herald a return to the militarism of the past, and would prove that the widespread fears of such a possibility were unnecessarily exaggerated.[9]

2. Strategic aid symbolizes the gradual weakening of the "separation of politics from economics" approach to foreign policy. In the first decades of the postwar period, Japan consciously avoided political entanglements in world affairs, concentrating almost exclusively on the promotion of economic relations with other nations. In a sense, the Japanese have always recognized the oneness of politics and economics; after all, that is precisely why they separated them in the first place. Today Japan consciously seeks a political role in international relations. Economic aid provides a nice blend of political objectives and economic means of obtaining those objectives.

Japan's relations with the Third World have moved gradually beyond the previously one-dimensional economics-first stance. The process has been slow. Tokyo has not jumped headlong into another region's political problems—nor is it likely to in the near future. In some areas Japan provides strategic assistance because of its interest in political and strategic developments. Japan has in these cases pondered and then dared. In other areas interest in political-strategic developments followed the extension of strategic aid to bolster the interests of Western friends. Japan has dared and must now ponder the consequences. But the long-term result of attention to and involvement in all of these areas may be the emergence of Japan as a truly global power.

3. Strategic aid both symbolizes and reinforces a gradual but steady globalization of Japanese diplomatic perspectives. The Japanese focused almost exclusively on Asia in economic aid policy during the early years. The government originally intended strategic uses of ODA as part of its Asia

policy as well. In the 1970s and 1980s Asia remains top priority, but approximately one third of bilateral assistance now flows beyond Asia.

Japan's selective but steady venture into non-Asian developing continents has focused attention on regional tensions and conflicts Japan may have tried to ignore or sidestep in previous eras. In the Middle East, Africa, and Latin America, Japan's use of aid takes the form of carrots to serve both Japanese and Western interests. But however Japan's global perspective and vision may widen, its global reach will be limited. Tokyo's influence will be used selectively, often ineffectively and often not at all. Japan cannot do that much in these areas. Its words and deeds will not be backed by military sanctions, its political leverage is weak and economic aid has its limits as a diplomatic tool. There will also be dangers—of being unwillingly dragged into other countries' squabbles; of being identified with unpopular, oppressive regimes; of being accused of interference in recipient nations' internal affairs; of enriching the ruling classes in developing countries; of exploiting the human and natural resources of the Third World. From a Japanese point of view, though, the potential rewards from a more stable Third World are great, and risk-taking is a price a global power must pay in a world of interdependence.

4. Strategic aid provides the Japanese with a means of demonstrating independence in foreign policy—but within the framework of allegiance to the Western alliance and the maintenance of close relations with recipient nations. "Independence," usually defined as independence from the United States, has been the needle in the haystack of Japanese foreign policy during the postwar era. Some have found an independent attitude during the early postwar period,[10] others see an independent streak all along (for example, in China policy), but most consider it a very recent phenomenon.[11]

In economic aid policy Japanese aid critics decried Tokyo's alleged surrogate role during the Vietnam conflict: Washington supplied the military punch, Tokyo the economic slap. Today some complain about the globalization of the surrogate role beyond Southeast Asia, insinuating that Japan lacks independent, indigenous reasons for aid-giving. But the distinction between surrogate and indigenous interests is artificial, for Japan pursues both indigenous interests and interests shared in common with Western nations and aid recipients.

The convergence of diplomatic independence, allegiance to Western allies, and commitment to close relations with recipients is most notable in the Asian region. Japan stresses its relations with neighboring nations more than with any other region. Japan, however, pursues its own course; it does not behave like a surrogate. Tokyo consistently reiterates its commitment to ASEAN as Japan's primary aid recipient; each year, one-third of total ODA is reserved for ASEAN nations. Yet Japan has risked ASEAN criticism in pursuing its interests in the region. Japan drew ASEAN's fire by increasing aid to Laos, elevating China as the largest bilateral ODA recipient in record time, accepting South Korean demands for $4 billion and for worrisome maneuvers toward Vietnam (restoring high-level contacts, pledging almost unlimited aid after a successful settlement of the Kampuchean problem and making unsolicited proposals to end the deadlock between Vietnam and ASEAN over Kampuchea). On the other hand Japan has held the line against U.S. suggestions that Japan reduce attention to Asia in favor of increased aid to other regions. In other words Japan would engage in diplomatic and aid policy activism in Asia without U.S. or European pressure in pursuit of indigenous interests. Japan does not wish to follow the advice of nineteenth-century philosopher Fukuzawa Yukichi to "escape from Asia and enter the West" ("Datsu-A, Nyu-O").

Beyond Asia, the picture is mixed. The Japanese initiated the globalization of aid policy in the 1970s for indigenous reasons, as a response to the energy crisis and not as a response to foreign pressure. With the advent of strategic aid in the late 1970s, Tokyo intended to restrict its use primarily to Asia. The Japanese did not initially expect the pace and scope of globalization of strategic aid to quicken and expand so dramatically. Coupled with the Japanese tendency to regard Latin America, Africa, and the Middle East as the "preserves" of the United States and West Europeans, aid beyond Asia seems to have received a strong American and European push.

In Latin America the shadow of the United States looms large over Japanese aid to the Caribbean Basin and Central America. That Japan would embark on an active aid program in Jamaica, El Salvador, Honduras, or Costa Rica (or curtail aid to Cuba and Nicaragua) without U.S. urging is difficult to believe. On the other hand Japan's concern over the debt crisis in Mexico, Brazil, and Argentina reflects its fear of a disruption, and perhaps destruction, of the international economic system that has served Japanese interests so well. Brazil and Peru share a special dimension in Japanese aid policy because of the large Japanese immigrant communities.

In Africa and the Middle East, aid to countries like Lebanon, Sudan, Chad, and Turkey represents a Japanese effort to support Western interests, especially those of the United States, France, and West Germany. The United States accords Egypt top priority (along with Israel) in aid policy, but until recent years, Cairo had consistently placed in the top 10 in Japan's aid policy as well. Western and Japanese interests in the Persian Gulf region coincide, and Japan would remain interested and involved even without Western pressure. Tokyo's recent exploration of ways to mitigate tensions between Iraq and Iran suggests a potential intermediary role not possible for the United States or European nations.

To be sure, Japan's "independent" aid diplomacy has been modest, tentative, and conditional. Initiatives have been compatible with Western political and strategic interests. However, the Japanese have not languished as prisoners of other nations' demands and interests. The Japanese have used aid as a relatively low-risk means of embarking on diplomatic initiatives that do not involve the same kinds of immediate costs endemic to military intervention and commitments. Strategic aid functions as a cautious first step toward the internationalization of Japanese foreign policy.

To those who question the pace of Japan's emergence as a global nation, the American experience may prove instructive. The United States achieved the status of a world class power around the turn of this century, but it required two world wars and a world depression to shake Americans from their basically isolationist, "fortress America" outlook. Americans historically and the Japanese recently have shared some similar attitudes toward the outside world: Both peoples remained skeptical of extensive foreign entanglements; they considered power politics a distasteful game played by other nations; and both felt that involvement abroad should be selective, limited, and preferably close to home, within their immediate geographic regions. American acceptance of global responsibilities evolved gradually, at a pace commensurate with perceived national capabilities and national will. By comparison, given the impact of World War II on Japanese attitudes toward "great powerism," Japan's internationalization is right on schedule through such means as strategic aid—but on its own schedule.

To those who question the direction of Japanese foreign policy, one should not expect the Japanese to follow in the footsteps of the United States. Japan is not likely to assume the role of the world's policeman. The Japanese feel ill at ease in a world of Realpolitik, if that world is defined by nation-states constantly seeking power, upholding the effectiveness of the use of force and relegating nonmilitary activities to the realm of "low" rather than "high politics." The Japanese would feel more at home in Keohane and Nye's world of "complex interdependence," in which the use of force is circumscribed and recognized as often ineffective or unusable, and in which international economic and other nonmilitary activities are regarded as "high politics."[12] These are the basic premises underlying the concept of comprehensive national security. But the world of complex interdependence remains an ideal type, as Keohane and Nye observe, as does the world of Realpolitik: "Sometimes, realist assumptions will be accurate, or largely accurate, but frequently, complex interdependence will provide a better portrayal of reality."[13]

In a hybrid world somewhere between Realpolitik and complex interdependence, strategic aid serves as a hybrid policy designed to avoid the dangers of a realist world the Japanese acknowledge but do not favor and to prepare for participation in an interdependent world they favor but do not yet see.

The Japanese have the ability to surprise. Few expected Japan to rise so quickly from the ashes of defeat and destruction following World War II. Few expected the economic miracle that catapulted Japan into a trillion dollar plus economy in a matter of decades. Few expected Japan to rejoin the ranks of great powers. And perhaps few today expect Japan to remain a great power without increasing its military capabilities commensurate with its economic strength. The Japanese plan otherwise: Maintain or improve economic strength, control and moderate military strength. If the Japanese manage to achieve and maintain great power status on that foundation, they may surprise us again with an achievement that would outshine even the remarkable economic miracle. And if strategic aid serves as a central pillar in the quest for that status, then the manner of giving will have indeed been worth more than the gift itself.

Notes

1. This is the view of Shinsuke Samejima, for example, in "Can Japan Steer Its Foreign Aid Policy Clear of Militarism?" *Japan Quarterly* (January–March 1982):33.

2. John White, *The Politics of Foreign Aid* (New York: St. Martin's Press, 1974), p. 20.

3. United States Department of State, Bureau of Public Affairs, *International Security and Economic Cooperation Program FY 1983*, March 1982, pp. 8–9.

4. Ryokichi Hirono, "Japan, the United States, and Development Assistance to Southeast Asia," in Michael Blaker, ed., *Development Assistance to Southeast Asia* (New York: Occasional Papers of the East Asian Institute Project on Japan and the United States in Multilateral Diplomacy, Columbia University, 1983), p. 96.

5. Robert A. Packenham, *Liberal America and the Third World* (Princeton, N.J.: Princeton University Press, 1973), p. 17.

6. Klaus Knorr, *The Power of Nations* (New York: Basic Books, 1975), p. 200.

7. Ibid., p. 172.

8. Ibid., p. 200–1.

9. J. W. M. Chapman, "Part Three: Dependence," in J. W. M. Chapman, R. Drifte, and I. T. M. Gow, *Japan's Quest for Comprehensive Security: Defence, Diplomacy and Dependence* (New York: St. Martin's Press, 1982), p. 235.

10. For example, see Martin E. Weinstein, *Japan's Postwar Defense Policy, 1947–1968* (New York: Columbia University Press, 1971).

11. Michael Yoshitsu dates it from 1973, in *Caught in the Middle East: Japan's Diplomacy in Transition* (Lexington, Mass.: Lexington Books, 1984).

12. Robert O. Keohane and Joseph S. Nye, *Power and Interdependence: World Politics in Transition* (Boston: Little, Brown, 1977), pp. 23–24.

13. Ibid., p. 24.

Bibliography

Selected Books

Akao, Nobutoshi, ed. *Japan's Economic Security.* New York: St. Martin's Press, 1983.

Anzen Hosho Kenkyukai. *Ekonomisuto ga Kaita Sogo Anzen Hosho no Kozu.* Tokyo: Nihon Seisansei Honbu, 1981.

Association for Promotion of International Cooperation. *The Developing Countries and Japan.* Tokyo, 1981.

————. *A Guide to Japan's Aid.* Tokyo, 1982.

Barnett, Robert W. *Beyond War: Japan's Concept of Comprehensive National Security.* Washington and New York: Pergamon Brassey's International Defense Publishers, 1984.

Black, Lloyd D. *The Strategy of Foreign Aid.* Princeton, N.J.: D. Van Nostrand, 1968.

Blaker, Michael, ed. *Development Assistance to Southeast Asia: The U.S. and Japanese Approaches.* New York: Occasional Papers of the East Asian Institute Project on Japan and the United States in Multilateral Diplomacy, 1983.

Chapman, J.W.M., R. Drifte, and I.T.M. Gow. *Japan's Quest for Comprehensive Security: Defence, Diplomacy, Dependence.* New York: St. Martin's Press, 1982.

Cunningham, George. *The Management of Aid Agencies.* London: Croom Helm, 1974.

Hasegawa, Sukehiro. *Japanese Foreign Aid; Policy and Practice.* New York: Praeger, 1975.

Heiwa Anzen Hosho Kenkyujo. *Ajia no Anzen Hosho.* Tokyo: Asagumo Shimbunsha, 1981.

Kaplan, Jacob J. *The Challenge of Foreign Aid.* New York: Praeger, 1971.

Knorr, Klaus. *The Power of Nations; The Political Economy of International Relations.* New York: Basic Books, 1975.

Knorr, Klaus, and Frank N. Trager. *Economic Issues and National Security.* Lawrence, Kan.: Allen Press, 1977.

Lee, Chae-Jin. *China and Japan: New Economic Diplomacy.* Stanford, Calif.: Hoover Institution Press, 1984.

Liska, George. *The New Statecraft; Foreign Aid in American Foreign Policy.* Chicago: The University of Chicago Press, 1960.

Loutfi, Martha F. *The Net Cost of Japanese Foreign Aid.* New York: Praeger, 1973.
Matsui, Ken. *Keizai Kyoryoku; Towareru Nihon no Keizai Gaiko.* Tokyo: Yuhikaku, 1983.
Montgomery, John D. *Foreign Aid in International Politics.* Englewood Cliffs, N.J.: Prentice-Hall, 1967.
Nagatomi, Yuichiro. *Kindai o Koete: Ko-Ohira Sori no Nokosareta Mono.* Vol. 2. Tokyo: Okura Zaimu Kyokai, 1983.
Nelson, Joan M. *Aid, Influence, and Foreign Policy.* New York: Macmillan, 1968.
Nishi, Kazuo. *Keizai Kyoryoku: Seiji Taikoku Nihon e no Michi.* Tokyo: Chuo Koron, 1970.
Nishihara, Masashi. *The Japanese and Sukarno's Indonesia: Tokyo-Jakarta Relations, 1951–1966.* Honolulu: University of Hawaii Press, 1976.
Ohlin, Goran. *Foreign Aid Policies Reconsidered.* Paris: OECD, 1966.
Otake, Hideo. *Nihon no Boei to Kokunai Seiji.* Tokyo: Sanichi, 1983.
Ozaki, Robert S., and Walter Arnold, eds. *Japan's Foreign Relations: A Global Search for Economic Security.* Boulder, Colo.: Westview Press, 1985.
Ozawa, Terutomo. *Multinationalism, Japanese Style: The Political Economy of Outward Dependency.* Princeton, N.J.: Princeton University Press, 1979.
Packenham, Robert A. *Liberal America and the Third World: Political Development Ideas in Foreign Aid and Social Science.* Princeton, N.J.: Princeton University Press, 1973.
Research Institute for Peace and Security. *Asian Security 1982.* Tokyo: Nikkei Business Publishing Company, 1982.
Rix, Alan. *Japan's Economic Aid.* New York: St. Martin's Press, 1980.
Shishido, Toshio. *Tonan Ajia Enjo o Kangaeru.* Tokyo: Toyo Keizai Shimposha, 1973.
Sogo Anzen Hosho Kenkyu Grupu. *Sogo Anzen Hosho Senryaku.* Tokyo: Okurasho Insatsu Kyoku, 1980.
Sogo Kenkyu Kaihatsu Kiko, and Nomura Sogo Kenkyusho. *21 Seiki ni Mukete no 'Nihon no Sogo Senryaku'; Kokusai Kankyo Oyobi Waga Kuni no Keizai-Shakai no Henka o Fumaeta Sogo Senryaku no Tenkai.* May 1977.
Tsurutani, Taketsugu. *Japanese Policy and East Asian Security.* New York: Praeger, 1981.
Waltz, Kenneth. *Foreign Policy and Democratic Politics.* Boston: Little, Brown, 1967.
White, John. *Japanese Aid.* London: Overseas Development Institute, 1974.
————. *The Politics of Foreign Aid.* New York: St. Martin's Press, 1964.
Yamamoto, Tsuyoshi. *Nihon no Keizai Enjo.* Tokyo: Sanseido, 1978.
Yasutomo, Dennis T. *Japan and the Asian Development Bank.* New York: Praeger Special Studies, 1983.
Yoshitsu, Michael. *Caught in the Middle East: Japan's Diplomacy in Transition.* Lexington, Mass.: Lexington Books, 1984.

Selected Articles

Aftàb, Mohammed. "Symbols, Not Substance." *Far Eastern Economic Review* (May 17, 1984): 66–68.

Ando, Hiroshi. "Japan's Budget: Leadership and Control." *JEI Report*, February 17, 1984.

Aoki, Minoru. "Bijon Naki Nihon no Keizai Enjo no Jittai." *Ajia* (May 1982): 74-82.

Aoki, Toshio. "Japan's Official Development Assistance to Asian Countries." *Journal of Japanese Trade and Industry* (May/June 1983): 59-61.

Arnold, Walter. "Japan and China." In Robert S. Ozaki and Walter Arnold, eds., *Japan's Foreign Relations: A Global Search for Economic Security*. Boulder, Colo.: Westview Press, 1985, pp. 102-18.

Atsumi, Keiko. "Japan Is No Exception to World Wide Trend of Declining Development Assistance." *Industrial Review of Japan 1983*, pp. 20-21.

Baba, Hiromasa. "Economic Cooperation with India and Pakistan: Nakasone's Visit Strengthens Bilateral Ties." *Look Japan*, July 10, 1984, pp. 19-20.

Brooks, William L., and Robert M. Orr, Jr. "Japan's Foreign Economic Assistance." *Asian Survey* (March 1985): 322-40.

Caldwell, J. Alexander. "The Evolution of Japanese Economic Cooperation, 1950-1970." In Harald B. Malmgren, ed., *Pacific Basin Development: The American Interests*. Lexington, Mass.: Lexington Books, 1972, pp. 61-80.

Campbell, William R. "Japan and the Middle East." In Robert S. Ozaki and Walter Arnold, eds., *Japan's Foreign Relations: A Global Search for Economic Security*. Boulder, Colo.: Westview Press, 1985, pp. 133-52.

Chinworth, Michael. "Japan and Latin America: Economic and Political Relations." *JEI Report*, April 5, 1985.

Choy, Jon. "Taking from Peter to Pay Paul: 1985 Japanese Fiscal Policy." *JEI Report*, May 24, 1985.

Curtis, Gerald L. "Japanese Security Policies and the United States." *Foreign Affairs* (Spring 1981): 852-74.

"Development: Japan's Foreign Aid." *Japan Times Weekly*, March 16, 1985, p. 7.

"The Economic Cooperation Budget for Fiscal 1983: Highest Annual Growth Allowed for Economic Cooperation Budget." *Look Japan*, April 10, 1983, pp. 12-13.

"Economic Ties with Africa." *Look Japan*, October 10, 1984, p. 5.

Elsbree, Willard H., and Khong Kim Hoong. "Japan and ASEAN." In Robert S. Ozaki and Walter Arnold, eds., *Japan's Foreign Relations: A Global Search for Economic Security*. Boulder, Colo.: Westview Press, 1985, pp. 119-32.

Eto, Shinkichi. "Recent Developments in Sino-Japanese Relations." *Asian Survey* (July 1980): 726-43.

"Government Position Behind Yen Loan Extension: A Growing Role of Yen Loans." *Look Japan*, April 10, 1984, pp. 10-11.

Hirono, Ryokichi. "A Decade of Development: The Mutual Dependence of Japan and the Third World Deepens." *Look Japan*, November 10, 1984, pp. 2-3, 4.

———. "Japan, the United States, and Development Assistance to Southeast Asia." In Michael Blaker, ed., *Development Assistance to Southeast Asia*. New York: Occasional Papers of the East Asian Institute, Columbia University, 1983, pp. 71-124.

Hoon, Shim Jae. "A Yen for a Thaw." *Far Eastern Economic Review* (January 27, 1981): 13-14.

Hosono, Akio. "Japan and Latin America." In Robert S. Ozaki and Walter Arnold, eds., *Japan's Foreign Relations: A Global Search for Economic Security*. Boulder, Colo.: Westview Press, 1985, pp. 200-26.

Ikeda, Yoshitaka. "Kyuzo suru Keizai Kyoryoku ni wa Nani o Nerau ka." *Akahata Hyoron Tokusha-ban,* November 16, 1981, pp. 12–17.

Ito, Soichiro. "The International Situation and Japan's Defense." *Asia Pacific Community* (Summer 1982): 1–13.

"Japan Hikes Aid, Moves to 2nd." *Japan Times Weekly,* June 29, 1985, p. 6.

"Japan's ODA Disbursements Reach Record Levels." *JEI Report,* June 21, 1985; pp. 4–5.

"Japanese and the Far Continent." *Look Japan,* October 10, 1984, pp. 4–5.

Kawai, Saburo. "Keizai Kyoryoku to Kaihatsu Enjo." In Hiromi Arisawa, ed., *Nihon Keizai to Anzen Hosho.* Tokyo: Tokyo Daigaku Shuppankai, 1981.

Kerns, Hikaru. "From Loan Recipient to Major Aid Supplier." *Far Eastern Economic Review* (September 27, 1984): 93–94.

Kim, Hong N. "Politics of Japan's Economic Aid to South Korea." *Asia Pacific Community* (Spring 1983): 80–102.

Kimura, Shuzo. "The Role of the Diet in Foreign Policy and Defense." In Francis R. Valeo and Charles E. Morrison eds., *The Japanese Diet and the U.S. Congress.* Boulder, Colo.: Westview Press, 1983, pp. 99–114.

Koshino, Yoshitaka, "Development Aid for Sub-Saharan Africa." *Look Japan,* October 10, 1984, pp. 17–19.

————. "Restoring Good Investments in Latin American Nations." *Look Japan,* March 10, 1985, pp. 16–17.

Liberal Democratic Party. Policy Affairs Research Council. Special Committee on Overseas Economic Cooperation. *Waga To no Keizai Kyoryoku Seisaku ni Tsuite.* Tokyo: Jiyu Minshuto Seimu Chosakai, 1983.

Matsumoto, Keiichi. "Economic Cooperation with Algeria, Morocco, Tunisia: Closer Ties with Maghreb Region." *Look Japan,* December 10, 1984, pp. 18–19.

————. "Economic Cooperation with Egypt: Mubarak's Visit Here Deepens Japan-Egypt Relations." *Look Japan,* May 10, 1983, pp. 20–21, 23.

————. "Japan-Egypt Economic Cooperation: Focus on Infrastructure for a Strategic Partner." *Look Japan,* June 10, 1984, pp. 14–16.

Matsumoto, Shigekazu. "Nihon no Enjo: Hikaku Yui o Ikase." *Boei to Kanzei,* January 1983, pp. 51–55.

Matsuura, Koichiro. "Japan's Cooperative Relations with ASEAN: Assistance Will Never Fail to Grow." *Mainichi Daily News,* September 30, 1981.

————. "Japan's Role in International Cooperation." *National Development,* September 1981, pp. 63–68.

————. "'Keizai Kyoryoku Taikoku Nihon' e no Michi." *Keizai to Gaiko* (March 1982): 14–27.

————. "Nichi-Doku Enjo Seisaku Kikaku Kyogi ni Shusseki Shite." *Kokusai Kyoryoku Tokubetsu Joho* (August 1981): 1–9.

————. "Saikin no Namboku Mondai no Doko to Nihon no Keizai Kyoryoku." *Keizai to Gaiko* (December 1982): 22–33.

————. "Senshin Sho-Koku no Saikin no Enjo Seisaku no Doko." *Kokusai Kaihatsu Janaru* (August 1981): 52–56.

————. "Waga Kuni no Keizai Kyoryoku no Arikata—Enjo Taisho Koku wa Dono Yoo na Kijun de Erabu ka." *Keizai to Gaiko* (March 1981): 24–33.

McKinlay, R.D., and R. Little. "A Foreign Policy Model of U.S. Bilateral Aid Allocation." *World Politics* (October 1977): 58–86.

Miyazawa, Shumitsu. "Japan-China Economic Cooperation: New Yen Credits for Infrastructure Development." *Look Japan,* May 10, 1984, pp. 16-17, 21.

Miyazawa, Shumitsu, and Shigemi Katabami, "Economic Cooperation with Thailand and the Philippines: Nakasone's Visit Strengthens Bonds." *Look Japan,* July 10, 1983, pp. 14-16.

Mochizuki, Mike M. "Japan's Search for Strategy." *International Security* (Winter 1983-84): 152-79.

Momoi, Makoto. "Are There Any Alternative Strategies for the Defense of Japan?" In Franklin Weinstein, ed., *U.S.-Japan Relations and the Security of East Asia: The Next Decade.* Boulder, Colo.: Westview Press, 1978, pp. 71-92.

Morley, James William. "A Time for Realism in the Military Defense of Japan." In Franklin Weinstein, ed., *U.S.-Japan Relations and the Security of East Asia: The Next Decade.* Boulder, Colo.: Westview Press, 1978, pp. 49-70.

Morris, David. "Japanese Investment in Africa." *New African* (May 1983): 39-40.

————. "Japanese Trade with Africa." *New African* (May 1983): 41-44.

Nakamura, Toshio. "Economic Cooperation: Supporting Thailand's National Development Plans." *Look Japan,* January 10, 1985, pp. 9, 11.

Nakaoka, San-eki. "Recent Economic Relations Between Japan and the Arab World." In *Mishima Symposium: Arab-Japanese Relations.* Tokyo: Japan National Committee for the Study of Arab-Japanese Relations, 1982, pp. 55-68.

————. "Studies on Egypt's Legal System Conducted by Japanese Bureaucrats in the Early Meiji Era." In *Arab-Japanese Relations: Tokyo Symposium.* Tokyo: Japan National Committee for the Study of Arab-Japanese Relations, 1980, pp. 135-40.

Nakasone, Yasuhiro. "Toward Comprehensive Security." *Japan Echo* 5, no. 4 (1978): 32-39.

Oda, Hideo, and Kazuyoshi Aoki. "Japan and Africa: Beyond the Fragile Partnership." In Robert S. Ozaki and Walter Arnold, eds., *Japan's Foreign Relations: A Global Search For Economic Security.* Boulder, Colo.: Westview Press, 1985, pp. 153-68.

Ogiso, Isamu. "Kisha no Me: ASEAN ni Furimawasareru na." *Mainichi Shimbun,* July 21, 1983.

Okawara, Yoshio. "The Underlying Concept in Japan's Defense Policy." *Asia Pacific Community* (Summer 1981): 28-33.

Okazaki, Hisahiko. "Improving Relations with South Korea: Chun, Nakasone Build Official Friendship, but Historical 'Perception Gap' Lingers On." *Look Japan,* October 10, 1984, pp. 2-3.

Okimoto, Daniel I. "The Economics of National Defense." In Daniel I. Okimoto, ed., *Japan's Economy: Coping with Change in the International Environment.* Boulder, Colo.: Westview Press, 1982, pp. 231-84.

Okita, Saburo. "Japan Should Rethink Its Aid to Southeast Asia." *Asian Wall Street Journal,* June 24-25, 1983.

Olsen, Edward A. "Japan and Korea." In Robert S. Ozaki and Walter Arnold, eds., *Japan's Foreign Relations: A Global Search for Economic Security.* Boulder, Colo.: Westview Press, 1985, pp. 169-86.

Orr, Robert M., Jr. "Help Is on the Way: An Analysis of the Aid Game." *Japan Times,* January 27, 1985, p. 12.

Palmer, Norman D. "Foreign Aid and Foreign Policy: The 'New Statecraft' Reassessed." *Orbis* (Fall 1969): 763–83.

Pye, Lucian W. "Soviet and American Styles in Foreign Aid." *Orbis* (Summer 1960): 159–73.

Ravenhill, John. "Japanese Aid to Africa." *New African* (May 1983): 40–41.

Rix, Alan. "ASEAN and Japan: More Than Economics." In Alison Broinowski, ed., *Understanding ASEAN*. London and Basingstoke: MacMillan Press, 1982, pp. 169–95.

Roscoe, Bruce. "An Argument over Aid—and What It Really Amounts To." *Far Eastern Economic Review* (June 13, 1985): 86–88.

Saeki, Kiichi. "Nihon No Anzen Hosho." In Hiromi Arisawa, ed., *Nihon Keizai to Anzen Hosho*. Tokyo: Tokyo Daigaku Shuppankai, 1981, pp. 39–63.

Samejima, Shinsuke. "Can Japan Steer Its Foreign Aid Policy Clear of Militarism?" *Japan Quarterly* (January-March, 1982): 30–38.

Shimomura, Norio. "Japan's Economic Cooperation with Latin America: Emphasis on Technical Cooperation and Large-Scale Development Projects." *Look Japan*, May 10, 1982, pp. 16–17.

Smith, Charles. "The Aid Dilemma." *Far Eastern Economic Review* (August 30, 1984): 64.

———. "Japanese Middle Man." *Far Eastern Economic Review* (September 29, 1984): 42–43.

Suzuki, Yuji. "Gunkaku to Fukyo no Naka no Keizai Kyoryoku." *Sekai* (July 1983): 52–65.

Taga, Hidetoshi. "Sengo Nihon no Keizai Enjo no Kiseki." *Ajia* (May 1982): 84–95.

Takubo, Tadae. "First Round of Nakasone's Diplomacy." *Asia Pacific Community* (Summer 1983): 1–10.

Tamagami, Masaaki. "Economic Cooperation with Sub-Saharan Countries: Credits Targeted at Creation of Infrastructure." *Look Japan*, September 10, 1982, pp. 16–17.

Wanner, Barbara. "Foreign Aid: Its Significance in Japanese Foreign Policy." *JEI Report* (July 2, 1981).

———. "Japan's Foreign Aid Policy: An Annual Update." *JEI Report*, September 14, 1984.

Weinstein, Martin E. "Japan's Defense Policy and the May 1981 Summit." *Journal of Northeast Asian Studies* (March 1982): 23–35.

Weintraub, Bernard. "Vietnam's Dominance in Laos Mars U.S. Efforts for Better Ties." *Asahi Evening News*, June 4, 1983.

Yamamoto, Teiichi. "White Paper: 'Present Status and Prospects for Economic Cooperation.'" *Look Japan*, March 10, 1983, pp. 18–19, 22.

Yanagi, Kenichi. "Japan Broadening Its Role in Field of Aid." *Japan Times*, January 8, 1983, p. 21.

———. "Japan's Economic Cooperation Taking New Direction. *Japan Times*, September 29, 1981.

———. "Konnichi no Sekai to Nihon no Enjo." *Kokusai Kyoryoku*, March 1983, pp. 6–9.

Yasuba, Yasukichi. "Economic Assistance Policy Needs Overhaul." *Look Japan*, April 10, 1982, p. 28.

Official Publications and Unpublished Manuscripts

Brooks, William L., and Robert M. Orr, Jr. "Japan's Foreign Economic Assistance."

Japan. Ministry of Foreign Affairs. "Anzen Hosho no Gunji-men to Hi-Gunji-men (Toku ni, Anzen Hosho Kara Mita Keizai Kyoryoku no Ichizuke." April 1982.

———. "Anzen Hosho Seisaku Kikaku Iinkai Dai 3 Kaigo Yoroku." April 28, 1982.

———. *Japan's Official Development Assistance 1984 Annual Report*. 1985.

———. "Nichi-Bei Kyodo Purojekuto no Tenkai." Undated manuscript.

———. Chosa Kikakubu, Kikakuka. *Anzen Hosho Mondai Handobukku*. March 1982.

———. *Diplomatic Bluebook, 1981 Edition: Review of Recent Developments in Japan's Foreign Relations*. Tokyo: Foreign Press Center/Japan, 1981.

———. Economic Cooperation Bureau. "Japanese Economic Cooperation." February 1, 1982.

———. Economic Cooperation Bureau. Economic Cooperation Evaluation Committee. *Keizai Kyoryoku Hyoka Hokokusho*. September 1982.

———. Keizai Kyoryoku Kyoku. Seisakuka. *Keizai Kyoryoku ni Kansuru Kihon Shiryo*. February 1983.

———. Economic Cooperation Bureau and Keizai Kyoryoku Kenkyukai. *Keizai Kyoryoku no Rinen—Seifu Kaihatsu Enjo wa Naze Okonau no ka*. Tokyo: Zaidan Hojin Kokusai Kyoryoku Suishin Kyokai, 1981.

———. Ministry of International Trade and Industry. *Economic Cooperation of Japan*. 1981.

———. *Keizai Kyoryoku no Genjo to Mondaiten*. Issues from 1976–1984.

———. Seisaku Kyoku. "Nichi-ASEAN Keizai Kankei no Kongo." *Boeki to Sangyo*, June 1983, pp. 29–33.

———. Office of the Prime Minister. Comprehensive National Security Study Group. *Report on Comprehensive National Security*. Tokyo: Office of the Prime Minister, 1980.

———. *Waga Kuni no Heiwa to Anzen ni Kansuru Yoron Chosa*. August 1982.

Matsumoto, Shigekazu. "Progress and Policy Formulation of Japan's External Assistance." Conference paper presented at "The U.S. Congress and the Japanese Diet: Conference on Comparative Studies in Foreign Policy." Honolulu. February 9–12, 1983.

Matsuura, Koichiro. "Sogo Anzen Hosho Seisaku Toshite no Keizai Kyoryoku." Speech delivered at Sogo Anzen Chosakai, Dai Yon-kai Kenkyukai. April 4, 1981.

Rinji Gyosei Chosakai Jimukyoku. *Rincho: Kihon Teigen; Rinji Gyosei Chosakai Dai 3-ji Toshin*. Tokyo: Gyosei Kanri Kenkyu Sentaa, 1982.

Takahama, Tatou, "Japan's Defense Policy." Paper presented at "The U.S. Congress and the Japanese Diet: Conference on Comparative Studies in Foreign Policy." Honolulu. February 9–12, 1983.

United States. Department of State. Bureau of Public Affairs. *International Security and Economic Cooperation Program FY1983*. March 1982.

————. Senate. Committee on Foreign Relations. Subcommittee on East Asian and Pacific Affairs. 97th Congress. *First Session on U.S. Policy Objectives in Southeast Asia and the Factors Which Shape Those Objectives. U.S. Policy in Southeast Asia.* July 15, 21, and 22, 1981. Washington, D.C.: U.S. Government Printing Office, 1981.

Periodicals and Journals

Asahi Shimbun

Asahi Evening News

Asia Pacific Community

Asian Survey

Asian Wall Street Journal

Asian Wall Street Journal Weekly

Daily Yomiuri

Far Eastern Economic Review

Foreign Affairs

Industrial Review of Japan

International Security

Japan Echo

Japan Economic Journal

Japan Quarterly

Japan Times

Japan Times Weekly

JEI Report

Journal of Japanese Trade and Industry

Journal of Northeast Asian Studies

Keizai to Gaiko

Kokusai Kaihatsu Janaru

Look Japan

Mainichi Daily News

Mainichi Shimbun

New African

New York Times

Nihon Keizai Shimbun

Tokyo Shimbun

World Politics

Yomiuri Shimbun

Interviews and Assistance

The following individuals were generous with both time and information at various stages in this project. Their institutional affiliations were those in effect at the time of the initial contact.

Aichi, Kazuo (Member of the Diet, Liberal Democratic Party)

Akita, Daisuke (Member of the Diet, Liberal Democratic Party)

Atoji, Hiroshi (International Bureau, Liberal Democratic Party)

Auer, James E. (U.S. Department of Defense)

Barnds, William (U.S. House of Representatives, Subcommittee on East Asia and the Pacific)

Bresnan, Jack (Asia Foundation and East Asian Institute, Columbia University)

Cohen, Donald (U.S. Agency for International Development) (Telephone)

Colbert, Evelyn (Carnegie Endowment for International Peace)

Eck, Sangsubana (Embassy of Thailand, Tokyo)

Foti, John (U.S. Agency for International Development Mission, Bangkok) (Correspondence)

Gyohten, Toyoo (Ministry of Finance)

Hagiwara, Yoshiyuki (Dokkyo University)

Hanada, Kiyoshi (Institute for Policy Research, Liberal Democratic Party)

Hattori, Norio (Ministry of Foreign Affairs)

Ikeda, Yoshitaka (Japan Communist Party)

Johnson, Samuel H. (University of Illinois) (Telephone and correspondece)

Kawaguchi, Yoriko (Office of the Prime Minister)

Kim, Woo Sang (Embassy of the Republic of Korea, Tokyo)

Kimura, Shuzo (Kobe University)

Kuromiya, Tokiyo (International Bureau, Liberal Democratic Party)

Locke, Mary (U.S. Senate, Subcommittee on East Asian and Pacific Affairs) (Telephone)

Matsuura, Koichiro (Ministry of Foreign Affairs)

Mizuki, Ikuo (Office of the Prime Minister)

Nakahira, Kosuke (Ministry of Finance)

Ng, Bak Hai (Embassy of Malaysia, Tokyo)

Nishihara, Masashi (National Defense Academy)

Nogami, Yoshiji (Ministry of Foreign Affairs)

Nozaki, Seigo (Ministry of Finance)

Ogura, Kazuo (Ministry of Foreign Affairs)

Ohashi, Yasushi (Overseas Economic Cooperation Fund)

Ohta, Hajime (Keidanren)

Okamoto, Sintaro (Policy Affairs Research Council, Liberal Democratic Party)

Orr, Robert M., Jr. (U.S. Agency for International Development)

Otsuji, Yoshihiro (Ministry of International Trade and Industry)

Rubenstein, Gregg (U.S. Department of Defense)

Sakurai, Toshihiro (Overseas Economic Cooperation Fund)

Sasanuma, Mitsuhiro (Overseas Economic Cooperation Fund)

Sato, Seizo, (Policy Affairs Research Council, Liberal Democratic Party)

Sayidiman, Suryohadiprojo (Embassy of Indonesia, Tokyo)

Schieck, Frederick W. (U.S. Agency for International Development)

Seligman, Albert (U.S. Department of State)

Seyama, Shuhei (Ministry of Agriculture, Forestry, and Fisheries)

Sezaki, Katsumi (Ministry of Foreign Affairs)

Sherry, Jerome (U.S. Agency for International Development)

Shibuya, Kunihiko (Member of the Diet, Clean Government Party)

Shiratori, Masayoshi (Ministry of Finance)

Shoesmith, Thomas (U.S. Department of State)

Sigur, Gaston (U.S. National Security Council)

Sneider, Richard (East Asian Institute, Columbia University)

Sorayouth, Prompoj (Embassy of Thailand, Tokyo)

Takahama, Tatou (Yomiuri Shimbun)

Takashima, Yushu (Ministry of Foreign Affairs)

Tanaka, Hitoshi (Embassy of Japan, Washington) (Telephone)

Tarumi, Hisami (International Bureau, Liberal Democratic Party)

Tsuchiya, Haruo (Ministry of Agriculture, Forestry, and Fisheries)

Valdes, Carlos T. (Embassy of the Philippines, Tokyo)

Watanabe, Roo (Member of the Diet, Democratic Socialist Party)

Yamamoto, Teiichi (Ministry of International Trade and Industry)

And the staff of the Institute of Developing Economies (Ajia Keizai Kenkyujo) in Tokyo.

Index

About the Author

Dennis T. Yasutomo is Five College Assistant Professor of Government at Smith College. He received his doctorate in political science from Columbia University. He was a Fulbright Scholar and served as a research associate and program officer/Japan at Columbia's East Asian Institute. He was appointed on two occasions as a visiting research fellow by the Institute of Developing Economies in Tokyo. Dr. Yasutomo is the author of *Japan and the Asian Development Bank* (Praeger, 1983).

Studies of the East Asian Institute

The Ladder of Success in Imperial China. Ping-ti Ho. New York: Columbia University Press, 1962.

The Chinese Inflation, 1937–1949. Shun-hsin Chou. New York: Columbia University Press, 1963.

Reformer in Modern China: Chang Chien, 1853–1926. Samuel Chu. New York: Columbia University Press, 1965.

Research in Japanese Sources: A Guide. Herschel Webb, with the assistance of Marleigh Ryan. New York: Columbia University Press, 1965.

Society and Education in Japan. Herbert Passin. New York: Teachers College Press, 1965.

Agricultural Production and Economic Development in Japan, 1873–1922. James I. Nakamura. Princeton: Princeton University Press, 1966.

Japan's First Modern Novel: Ukigumo of Futabatei Shimei. Marleigh Ryan. New York: Columbia University Press, 1967.

The Korean Communist Movement, 1918–1948. Dae-Sook Suh. Princeton: Princeton University Press, 1967.

The First Vietnam Crisis. Melvin Gurtov. New York: Columbia University Press, 1967.

Cadres, Bureaucracy and Political Power in Communist China. A. Doak Barnett. New York: Columbia Unversity Press, 1968.

The Japanese Imperial Institution in the Tokugawa Period. Herschel Webb. New York: Columbia University Press, 1968.

Higher Education and Business Recruitment in Japan. Koya Azumi. New York: Columbia University Press, 1969.

The Communists and Peasant Rebellions: A Study in the Rewriting of Chinese History. James P. Harrison, Jr. New York: Atheneum, 1969.

How the Conservatives Rule Japan. Nathaniel B. Thayer. Princeton: Princeton University Press, 1969.

Aspects of Chinese Education. C.T. Hu, ed. New York: Teachers College Press, 1970.

Documents of Korean Communism, 1918–1948. Dae-Sook Suh. Princeton: Princeton University Press, 1970.

Japanese Education: A Bibliography of Materials in the English Language. Herbert Passin. New York: Teachers College Press, 1970.

Economic Development and the Labor Market in Japan. Koji Taira. New York: Columbia University Press, 1970.

The Japanese Oligarchy and the Russo-Japanese War. Shumpei Okamoto. New York: Columbia University Press, 1970.

Imperial Restoration in Medieval Japan. H. Paul Varley. New York: Columbia University Press, 1971.

Japan's Postwar Defense Policy, 1947–1968. Martin E. Weinstein. New York: Columbia University Press, 1971.

Election Campaigning Japanese Style. Gerald L. Curtis. New York: Columbia University Press, 1971.

China and Russia: The "Great Game". O. Edmund Clubb. New York: Columbia University Press, 1971.

Money and Monetary Policy in Communist China. Katharine Huang Hsiao. New York: Columbia University Press, 1971.

The District Magistrate in Late Imperial China. John R. Watt. New York: Columbia University Press, 1972.

Law and Policy in China's Foreign Relations: A Study of Attitudes and Practice. James C. Hsiung. New York: Columbia University Press, 1972.

Pearl Harbor as History: Japanese–American Relations, 1931–1941. Dorothy Borg and Shumpei Okamoto, eds., with the assistance of Dale K.A. Finlayson. New York: Columbia University Press, 1973.

Japanese Culture: A Short History. H. Paul Varley. New York: Praeger, 1973.

Doctors in Politics: The Political Life of the Japan Medical Association. William E. Steslicke. New York: Praeger, 1973.

The Japan Teachers Union: A Radical Interest Group in Japanese Politics. Donald Ray Thurston. Princeton: Princeton University Press, 1973.

Japan's Foreign Policy, 1868–1941: A Research Guide. James William Morley, ed. New York: Columbia University Press, 1974.

Palace and Politics in Prewar Japan. David Anson Titus. New York: Columbia University Press, 1974.

The Idea of China: Essays in Geographic Myth and Theory. Andrew March. Devon, England: David and Charles, 1974.

Origins of the Cultural Revolution. Roderick MacFarquhar. New York: Columbia University Press, 1974.

Shiba Kokan: Artist, Innovator, and Pioneer in the Westernization of Japan. Calvin L. French. Tokyo: Weatherhill, 1974.

Insei: Abdicated Sovereigns in the Politics of Late Heian Japan. G. Cameron Hurst. New York: Columbia University Press, 1975.

Embassy at War. Harold Joyce Noble. Frank Baldwin, Jr., ed. and intro. Seattle: University of Washington Press, 1975.

Rebels and Bureaucrats: China's December 9ers. John Israel and Donald W. Klein. Berkeley: University of California Press, 1975.

Deterrent Diplomacy. James William Morley, ed. New York: Columbia University Press, 1976.

House United, House Divided: The Chinese Family in Taiwan. Myron L. Cohen. New York: Columbia University Press, 1976.

Escape from Predicament: Neo-Confucianism and China's Evolving Political Culture. Thomas A. Metzger. New York: Columbia University Press, 1976.

Cadres, Commanders, and Commissars: The Training of the Chinese Communist Leadership, 1920–45. Jane L. Price. Boulder, Colo.: Westview Press, 1976.

Sun Yat-Sen: Frustrated Patriot. C. Martin Wilbur. New York: Columbia University Press, 1977.

Japanese International Negotiating Style. Michael Blaker. New York: Columbia University Press, 1977.

Contemporary Japanese Budget Politics. John Creighton Campbell. Berkeley: University of California Press, 1977.

The Medieval Chinese Oligarchy. David Johnson. Boulder, Colo.: Westview Press, 1977.

The Arms of Kiangnan: Modernization in the Chinese Ordnance Industry, 1860–1895. Thomas L. Kennedy. Boulder, Colo.: Westview Press, 1978.

Patterns of Japanese Policymaking: Experiences from Higher Education. T.J. Pempel. Boulder, Colo.: Westview Press, 1978.

The Chinese Connection: Roger S. Greene, Thomas W. Lamont, George E. Sokolsky, and American–East Asian Relations. Warren I. Cohen. New York: Columbia University Press, 1978.

Militarism in Modern China: The Career of Wu P'ei-Fu, 1916–1939. Odoric Y.K. Wou. Folkestone, England: Dawson, 1978.

A Chinese Pioneer Family: The Lins of Wu-Feng. Johanna Meskill. Princeton: Princeton University Press, 1979.

Perspectives on a Changing China. Joshua A. Fogel and William T. Rowe, eds. Boulder, Colo.: Westview Press, 1979.

The Memoirs of Li Tsung-Jen. T.K. Tong and Li Tsung-Jen. Boulder, Colo.: Westview Press, 1979.

Unwelcome Muse: Chinese Literature in Shanghai and Peking, 1937–1945. Edward Gunn. New York: Columbia University Press, 1979.

Yenan and the Great Powers: The Origins of Chinese Communist Foreign Policy. James Reardon-Anderson. New York: Columbia University Press, 1980.

Uncertain Years: Chinese-American Relations, 1947–1950. Dorothy Borg and Waldo Heinrichs, eds. New York: Columbia University Press, 1980.

The Fateful Choice: Japan's Advance into South-East Asia. James William Morley, ed. New York: Columbia University Press, 1980.

Tanaka Giichi and Japan's China Policy. William F. Morton. Folkestone, England: Dawson, 1980; New York: St. Martin's Press, 1980.

The Origins of the Korean War: Liberation and the Emergence of Separate Regimes, 1945–1947. Bruce Cumings. Princeton: Princeton University Press, 1981.

Class Conflict in Chinese Socialism. Richard Curt Kraus. New York: Columbia University Press, 1981.

Education under Mao: Class and Competition in Canton Schools. Jonathan Unger. New York: Columbia University Press, 1982.

Private Academies of Tokugawa Japan. Richard Rubinger. Princeton: Princeton University Press, 1982.

Japan and the San Francisco Peace Settlement. Michael M. Yoshitsu. New York: Columbia University Press, 1982.

New Frontiers in American–East Asian Relations: Essays Presented to Dorothy Borg. Warren I. Cohen, ed. New York: Columbia University Press, 1983.

The Origins of the Cultural Revolution: II, The Great Leap Forward, 1958–1960. Roderick MacFarquhar. New York: Columbia University Press, 1983.

The China Quagmire: Japan's Expansion on the Asian Continent, 1933–1941. James William Morley, ed. New York: Columbia University Press, 1983.

Fragments of Rainbows: The Life and Poetry of Saito Mokichi, 1882–1953. Amy Vladeck Heinrich. New York: Columbia University Press, 1983.

The U.S.–South Korean Alliance: Evolving Patterns of Security Relations. Gerald L. Curtis and Sung-joo Han, eds. Lexington, Mass.: Lexington Books, 1983.

Japan and the Asian Development Bank. Dennis Yasutomo. New York: Praeger Publishers, 1983.

Discovering History in China: American Historical Writing on the Recent Chinese Past. Paul A. Cohen. New York: Columbia University Press, 1984.

The Foreign Policy of the Republic of Korea. Youngnok Koo and Sungjoo Han, eds. New York: Columbia University Press, 1984.

Japan Erupts: The London Naval Conference and the Manchurian Incident. James W. Morley, ed. New York: Columbia University Press, 1984.

Japanese Culture. 3rd. ed. rev. Paul Varley, Honolulu: University of Hawaii Press, 1984.

Japan's Modern Myths: Ideology in the Late Meiji Period. Carol Gluck. New York: Columbia University Press, 1985.

Shamans, Housewives, and Other Restless Spirits. Laurel Kendall. Honolulu: University of Hawaii Press, 1985.

Human Rights in Contemporary China. R. Randle Edwards, Louis Henkin, and Andrew J. Nathan. New York: Columbia University Press, 1986.